the BUSINESS START-UP KIT

Steven D. Strauss

Dearborn™
Trade Publishing
A **Kaplan Professional** Company

Vice President and Publisher: Cynthia A. Zigmund
Editorial Director: Donald J. Hull
Senior Acquisitions Editor: Jean Iversen
Senior Project Editor: Trey Thoelcke
Interior Design: Lucy Jenkins
Cover Design: KTK Design Associates
Typesetting: the dotted i

Published by Dearborn Trade Publishing, a Kaplan Professional Company

Printed in the United States of America

03   04   05   10   9   8   7   6   5   4   3   2   1

Library of Congress Cataloging-in-Publication Data
Strauss, Steven D., 1958–
     The business start-up kit / Steven D. Strauss.
         p.   cm.
     Includes index.
     ISBN 0-7931-6027-8
     1. New business enterprises—Management.   2. New business enterprises—United States—Management.   3. Entrepreneurship.   4. Success in business.
     I. Title.
     HD62.5 .S79 2003
     658.1′1—dc21

                                                                          2002014170

Dedication

For M, with love

Contents

Preface

Your own successful business can be many things. It can be your meal ticket, ensuring the economic health of you and your family. It can be your source of creativity, giving you an outlet for all of those ideas you have. It can be your security, the comfort that comes from knowing that there is no boss who can fire you. It can even be your pride and joy, an accomplishment that you point to with satisfaction, knowing that you alone created it out of whole cloth.

But more than anything else, I think that owning your own business and being an entrepreneur is about freedom. Yes, the money that comes from a successful business is great. And yes, being energized and enthused about your day is special. Being free is priceless. If you do it right, you are free to start whatever sort of business you want. You are free to start it where you want, and free to work the hours you choose. You are free to make as much money as you are capable of, without yearly limits or performance reviews.

But you will notice that all this only comes about *if you do it right*. When you choose to become an entrepreneur, there are no guarantees. In large part, whether you succeed or fail is up to you. So, how do you do it right? Read this book. It is dedicated to helping you succeed. And unlike other start-your-own-business books on the market, what sets this book apart is that it offers a *model* of business success, a simple model that is easily duplicated.

It might help to think of your business as having two parts. The first part is found in Chapters 1, 2, and 3 of this book—choosing and doing something that you love to do. That is the "technical" aspect of the business. The dentist fills the cavities, the photographer takes the pictures. Practically every business is set up to allow the owner to make money doing some sort of technical work that he or she loves.

The second part of your business is everything else—the actual running of the business itself. That is found in the rest of this book, Chapters 4 through 20. The dentist must network and bring in new clients, and the photographer must get referrals, bill customers, and generate leads. There are myriad things that go into running the actual business, aside from doing the "thing" that you love to do. When I talk about a model of business success, it is all of these other things to which I am referring.

The vast majority of this book is dedicated to teaching you this second part of business. If the dentist and photographer follow the model laid out in this book, they will be free to spend more time doing what it is they love, rather than worrying about the business. Do it right and the business will take care of itself, and you, in turn, will be free. You can plug almost any "technical" job into this business model and it would work.

The model is neither complicated nor complex. It is simple, easy, and fun. Learn it and free yourself up to grow, make more money, and do what it is you love. When you learn how to run your business properly, you get to a point where the world will be paying you to do what you love most. And that, as Alan Ginsberg once observed, is the real trick of life.

Acknowledgments

I would like to thank Jean Iversen for her patience and understanding. I would also like to thank Maria, Jillian, Sydney, and Mara.

I

Business Overview

This section gives you a broad overview of business in general and explores some ideas about what sort of business might be best for you. It's all here—home-based businesses, franchises, starting your own business from scratch, buying an existing business.

1

Business Overview

Congratulations! The decision to start your own business can be one of the best you will ever make in your life. Owning your own business should be an exhilarating, inspiring, grand adventure; one full of new sights and experiences, delicious highs and occasional lows, tricky paths and, hopefully, big open skys.

But to ensure that your business journey will be a fruitful one, it is important to understand all that becoming an entrepreneur entails. Therefore, in Part I, especially in this chapter, you will get a broad overview of business and its many forms and possibilities.

Pros and Cons

Many people start their business adventure dreaming of riches and freedom. And while both are certainly possible, the first thing to understand is that there are tradeoffs when you decide to start a business. Difficult bosses, annoying coworkers, peculiar policies, demands upon your time, and limits on how much money you can make are traded for independence, creativity, opportunity, and power. But by the same token, you also swap a regular paycheck and benefits for no paycheck and no benefits. A life of security, comfort, and regularity is traded for one of uncertainty.

There are definitely pros and cons to starting your own business. To be more precise, the benefits of starting a business include:

- *Control.* Even if you like your boss and your job, the possibility remains that you can be laid off at any time. That boss you like so much can be transferred. Your company can go bankrupt. So one advantage of starting your own business is that you are more in control of your work and career. And while that may be comforting, you should also realize that with that control will come increased responsibility and a new set of demands. As the boss, the buck must stop with you. You are the one who has to meet payroll. You are the one who has to make sure that clients and customers are happy. You are the one who must hire and fire the employees. It is not always easy, and you can bet that there will certainly be times when you will look fondly back on your days as an employee, when you had far less responsibility and control.

- *Money.* Many people choose to start their own business for the simple reason that they think that they are worth more money than they are making or they want the chance to provide a better life for their family. There is usually a limit to how much money you can make when you are an employee. The good news is that when you are the employer, the entrepreneur, the boss, there are far fewer limits. That can be a good or bad thing; you may make a fortune, or you may go bust. If this kind of uncertainty appeals to you, good, because it is what you will be getting if you start your own business.

- *Creativity and independence.* If you feel stagnant in your current job, you won't feel stagnant for long if you start a business. Running your own business may require you to be the marketing wizard, salesman, bookkeeper, secretary, and president all rolled into one. It is a hectic life. But you may not mind that. It's kind of like the Calvin and Hobbes cartoon in which Calvin's mother tells him to make his bed. Calvin decides to build a robot to make the bed for him. When Hobbes asks, "Isn't making the robot more work than making the bed?" Calvin answers, "It's only work if someone makes you do it!" The same holds true when the business is yours—it often doesn't feel like work because no one is making you do it.

- *Freedom.* Working at your own business gives you the flexibility to decide when and where you will work. You decide your hours and place of business. The freedom that comes with being your own boss, where no one can tell you what to do or how to do it, may be the best thing about being an entrepreneur.

But there are also downsides to starting your own business:

- *Uncertainty.* As indicated, the life of an entrepreneur is not necessarily an easy one. Is it fun? Yes. Is it challenging, exciting, and spontaneous? You bet. But it is not easy. The hardest part of being in business for yourself is that there is no steady source of income; a paycheck does not come every two weeks.
- *Risk.* What is an entrepreneur? An entrepreneur is someone who is *willing to take a risk with money to make money.* Not all entrepreneurial ventures are successful. The willingness to take a smart, calculated risk is the hallmark of a smart entrepreneur. But even calculated risks are still risks. You could make a million or you could go bankrupt.
- *Lack of structure.* Many people like the structure of working for someone else. They know what is expected of them and what they need to accomplish each day. This is not true when you work for yourself. The work is very unpredictable.

You need to consider carefully both the risks and rewards of entrepreneurship before deciding to jump in. It is easy to become infatuated with the idea of owning your own business. But if you are going to do it right, if you are going to be successful, you need to take emotion out of the equation. You have to begin to think like a businessman, consider the risks, and make an informed, intelligent, calculated decision.

Do You Have What It Takes?

Considering the pros and cons of this venture is not enough. Making the decision to leave your job and start a business is monumental. Even if starting a business seems like a great idea, despite the drawbacks, the question remains: How do you know if you are cut out to be an entrepreneur? Do you have what it takes? In order to assist you, answer the questions in the following quiz. It will help you evaluate your qualifications.

As you answer the questions, be sure to be perfectly honest. There is no need to get every question "right." Businesspeople come in all shapes, sizes, temperaments, and skill levels. Thus, no test can determine if you are perfectly suited to be an entrepreneur. But this test will help you realize some of the skills necessary to start your own business. You will only be hurting yourself and your business if you pretend to have skills you don't possess.

Assessing Yourself

1. Are you a self-starter?
   a) Yes, I like to do things on my own.
   b) If someone helps me get started, I will definitely follow through.
   c) Most of the time, I would rather follow than lead.

2. How do you feel about taking risks?
   a) I really like the feeling of being a bit on the edge.
   b) Calculated risks are acceptable at times.
   c) I like the tried and true.

3. Are you a leader?
   a) I usually get people to go along when I initiate something.
   b) I can give the orders if I have to.
   c) I let someone else get things moving, then I take part if I feel like it.

4. Do you like to assume responsibility?
   a) Yes, I enjoy taking charge of things and seeing them through.
   b) I'll take over if I have to, but would rather let someone else be responsible.
   c) There's always some eager beaver around wanting to show how smart he is. I say let him.

5. How organized are you?
   a) I like to have a plan before I start.
   b) Being well organized isn't my strongest suit, but I can do it when necessary.
   c) I just like to take things as they come.

6. How hard are you willing to work?
   a) I can stay motivated as long as necessary.
   b) I'll work hard for a while, but when I've had enough, that's it.
   c) I think many other things are more important than work.

7. Are you decisive?
   a) I can make up my mind in a hurry if I have to.
   b) If I have to make up my mind quickly, I do, but I don't like it.
   c) I don't like to be the one to decide things.

8. Can you live with uncertainty?
   a) Yes.
   b) I can if I have to, but I don't like it.
   c) No, I like knowing what to expect.

9. Can you stick with it?
   a) If I make up my mind to do something, I don't let anything get in the way.
   b) Usually.
   c) If things don't go right, I may just quit.

10. How good is your health?
    a) I never run down!
    b) I have enough energy for most of the things I want to do.
    c) I run out of energy sooner than most of my friends.

11. Are you competitive?
    a) You bet.
    b) When I need to be, I can be.
    c) Not really, my nature is more laid-back.

12. Do you have a lot of willpower and self-discipline?
    a) Yes.
    b) I am disciplined when I need to be.
    c) Not really.

13. Do you plan ahead?
    a) In my book, failure to plan is planning to fail.
    b) Planning is important, but so is spontaneity.
    c) I take one day at a time and let life take me where it will.

14. Are you creative?
    a) Yes I am. I am always thinking up new ideas.
    b) I have an occasional brainstorm.
    c) No, not really.

15. Can you live without structure?
    a) Yes.
    b) Actually, the idea of living without a regular job or paycheck makes me nervous.
    c) No, I like routine and structure in my life.

If you answered "a" on more than half of the questions, you have the personality needed to run your own business. If most of your answers were "b," you're likely to encounter more trouble than you may want.

If you have several "c" answers, then you are not quite ready to start your own business. But that does not mean that you can't *get* ready. While certain aspects of entrepreneurship are innate (the willingness to take a risk, for example), many are learned (such as knowing how to conduct market research). If the results of this quiz tell you to slow down, that is good. You can always take business classes, read more books, or listen to business tapes in order to learn more. Another option would be to get a partner who has the skills you lack. There are many ways to start your own business, and if you are not ready now, it does not mean you will never be ready.

■ Real Life Example

During World War II, a rubber shortage in the United States necessitated that the U.S. War Productions Board request that American companies try to create a synthetic rubber. In one of its experiments in support of this request, General Electric ended up with a pliable goo that, while not rubber, was interesting. Not knowing what to do with the stuff, GE sent it to academics all over the world, looking for suggestions. No one could think of a scientific use for the goo.

A few years after the war, a Harvard professor who had received some of the stuff earlier brought it out as a conversation piece at a cocktail party he was having. A guest at the party, a broke entrepreneur named Peter Hodgson, saw the adults playing with the stuff and had an idea. Despite being deeply in debt, Hodgson borrowed $150 and bought 21 pounds of the stuff along with the patent rights from GE. He started his own business in which he sold the goo packaged in small amounts in little plastic eggs. He named it Silly Putty.

Getting Started

Once you have decided that starting a business is right for you despite the risks, the question becomes: What's next? People often love the idea of starting a business but get bogged down in the actual nitty gritty of just how to do it. It might help to know that no matter what type of business you decide to start, the essential steps are the same. Different businesses will have slightly different paths but, *generally speaking*, most businesses follow a formulaic path. While this formula will be discussed in much more detail throughout this book, it will be helpful to have a road map to show you where you are headed.

Step 1: Personal Evaluation

You need to begin by taking stock of yourself and your situation in order to figure out which sort of business is best for you. Why do you want to start a business? Is it money, freedom, creativity, or some other reason? What do you bring to the table? What skills do you have? What industries do you know best? Would you want to provide a service or a product? What do you like to do? How much capital do you have to risk? Will it be a full-time or a part-time venture? Will you have employees? The answers to these types of questions will help you narrow your focus and pick a business. The rest of this chapter will help you do that.

Step 2: Analyze the Industry

Once you decide on a business that fits your goals and lifestyle, you will need to evaluate your idea. Who will buy your product or service? Who will be your competitors?

Step 3: Draft a Business Plan

If you will be seeking outside financing, a business plan is a necessity. But even if you are going to finance the venture yourself, a business plan will help you figure out how much money you will need to get started, what tasks need to be done when, and where you are headed.

Step 4: Make It Legal

There are several ways to form your business. It could be a sole proprietorship, a partnership, or a corporation. Although incorporating can be expensive, it is usually well worth the money. A corporation becomes a separate legal entity that is legally responsible for the business. If something goes wrong, you cannot be held personally liable. Chapter 7 discusses this in detail.

Once you form your business, you also need to get the proper business licenses and permits. Depending on the business, you may have to deal with city, county, or state regulations, permits, and licenses. This would also be the time to check into any insurance you may need for the business and find a good accountant.

Step 5: Get Financed

Depending on the size of your venture, you may need to seek financing from an "angel" or from a venture capital firm. Most small businesses begin with private financing from credit cards, personal loans, help from the family, second mortgages, savings, etc. As a rule of thumb, in addition to your start-up costs, you should have at least six months' worth of your family's budget in the bank.

Step 6: Set Up Shop

Find a location. Negotiate leases. Buy inventory. Get the phones installed. Have stationery printed. Hire staff. Set your prices. Throw a grand opening party.

Step 7: Trial and Error

It will take a while to figure out what works and what does not. Follow your business plan, but be open and creative. Advertise! Don't be afraid to make a mistake. And above all, have a ball—running your own business is one of the great joys in life!

Picking the Right Business

You already may know which type of business you want to start. If so, you get to pass Go, collect $200, and skip this section. But if you are not yet sure exactly which sort of business is right for you, then read on.

There are few times in life when the stars align themselves just right to allow you to go into business for yourself *and* pick the exact business you

---

✎ **Checklist for Starting Your Own Business**

- ☐ Complete a personal evaluation
- ☐ Analyze the industry
- ☐ Make the business legal
- ☐ Draft a business plan
- ☐ Get financed
- ☐ Set up shop
- ☐ Conduct business by trial and error

---

want. Usually, money is tight, the time is wrong, your wife is pregnant, or some other reason is preventing you from choosing the right business. Consider this a rare, golden opportunity and choose your business with care.

How do you go about choosing a business? There are many ways. Some people do something they know how to do well, and that's usually a fine idea. The main consideration for others is that their business has a high profit margin; again, not a bad idea. Still others want a business that is hot and trendy. This is not such a great idea.

There are always businesses that you can start on the cusp of a wave. A few years ago, you might have considered an e-commerce Web site. While this is still not a bad idea, it is definitely harder to make money in cyberspace these days. The problem with this idea is that waves crash. Starting a business based on a trend can be a recipe for disaster.

Instead, you should ask yourself the following five questions. The answers to these questions will be much more helpful than any list of hot businesses.

1. *What is something that I do well that I like to do?* As in life, we tend to succeed and do well when we are engaged in something that we really enjoy. Your business should be no different. Richard Branson started Virgin Music, not because he thought music would be hot, but because he loved music. Bill Gates started Microsoft because he

loved working with computers. As the title of a book says, do what you love, the money will follow.

2. *Is there a market for this business?* Let's say that the thing you love doing is gardening. Well, there is no shortage of businesses that revolve around that concept, such as nurseries and landscaping. But what if the thing you love most is nineteenth-century Danish architecture? However interesting it may be to you, you don't have a business if no one is willing to pay you for your expertise. So you have to be realistic—there must be a market willing to buy what you want to offer. Chapter 5 discusses how to do this in detail.

3. *Can I afford to start this business?* Some businesses are very inexpensive to start, most notably, home-based businesses. Others can be quite expensive. A nursery can easily cost $75,000 to create and stock. Buying into a well-known franchise can cost over $1 million. In addition to picking a business that you like for which you have a market, you also must make sure that it is one you can afford to start. This is discussed in detail later in this chapter.

4. *What will distinguish my business?* Your business must offer something unique if you are to attract customers. After all, they already shop somewhere else. Why will they choose to buy from you? You must offer better quality, cheaper prices, a more convenient location, better service, a unique product—something that makes you stand out from the crowd.

5. *Can I make a profit?* Whatever business you start, whatever product or service you sell, you have to be able to sell it at a price high enough to make a profit, but low enough that people will buy it. Setting this price is not always an easy task. Why do so many stores in expensive malls go out of business? Because often their overhead is too high, despite having a great concept. So before jumping into a business, crunch some numbers.

Although all of these issues are important, they should point toward one direction, namely, your passion. As you know, working with passion is one of the great joys in life. This is even more true when choosing a business. This business is going to become your baby. You will love it, care for it, nurse it along, and obsess over it. You will also be putting an extraordinary number of hours into it. You will be working at it all day, every day, hopefully for many years. Unless you love it deeply and are passionate about it, working so hard will be difficult.

✎ What Type of Business Should You Start?

Completing the following statements should help guide you to choosing an appropriate business.

I am happiest when I _____ .

I feel excited when I _____ .

If money were not an issue, I would _____ .

The best advice I ever received was _____ .

The best thing I ever did was _____ .

Work is best when _____ .

Life is best when _____ .

My hidden talent is _____ .

My purpose is _____ .

I have the most fun at work when I _____ .

The skills I most like using at work are _____ .

What people admire about me is _____ .

I am best at _____ .

The training I had that can help me is _____ .

Making the Decision

Deciding on an area that you love is only the first step when choosing a business to start. The rest of the required analysis is much more left-brained, more analytical. It consists of two steps:

1. Looking at how much you have to invest
2. Conducting market research

Analyzing Your Start-Up Costs

As important as it is to choose a business you will love, the business you pick must be one you can afford. While Chapter 9 discusses many ways to get the money you will need to start your business, you probably already have a fairly good idea how much you will have to get started. Needless to say, the business you choose must fit within those parameters.

Essentially, there are two types of businesses: service-based businesses and product-based businesses. Of the two, service businesses are far less expensive to start. If you open an accounting firm, for example, all you may need to get started is letterhead, an office, and a computer. On the other hand, if you want to start a computer store, you need to have inventory, shelving, fixtures, and display cases, not to mention retail space, a security system, and a sales staff.

One of the first things you must do is analyze your start-up costs to determine if you can afford to start the business that you love. Again, Chapter 9 will walk you through the process of determining how much money you will need to get started, but as you go about deciding what sort of business to start, keep in mind financial considerations.

Conducting Market Research

The other aspect of choosing the right business is making sure that there is a need for the business you want to start. There are few things worse in life than putting a lot of money, time, and effort into creating a new business, only to find that there is no market for what you are selling. Chapter 5 will help you understand how to conduct market research.

The important thing is that you choose a business that fits your personality, is something you love, and can be successfully implemented with the resources available to you. If that means scaling your idea back a bit in the beginning, that's fine. Once you get your baby off the ground, you can grow as much as you are able.

Overcoming Fear

No one ever said taking the leap was easy. Fun, exciting, inspiring, and maybe even a little nauseating? Yes. But easy? No. Starting your own business is a big step worthy of a second look. Whether you succeed or fail, every aspect of your life—from bank accounts to friendships—is affected. Although fear can be debilitating, avoidance is not the answer. Here are seven tips to help you overcome fear and get started living the dream:

1. *Remember that you can start slowly.* Quitting a nine-to-five job one day and starting a business the next would give anyone nightmares. You don't have to do it that way if you don't want to. Making a gradual transition gives you time to think, plan, and work on potential problems, which should help lessen your anxiety.

2. *Help is available.* And much of this help is free. The Small Business Administration, your friends, Web sites, the local chamber of commerce, and business associates will be available to help you along the way.

3. *Plan.* Nothing beats preparation to quell the panicky feelings that can keep entrepreneurs awake at night. "A well-thought-out business plan can go a long way toward helping alleviate start-up fears," says Mark Sobel, director of Small Business Development at the Stanley Entrepreneurial Center.

4. *Expect the unexpected.* Unless you are blessed with unlimited monetary resources, starting a business means taking a financial risk. Although you may not be able to keep all problems at bay, you can accept the reality that being in business brings risks along with the rewards. That's the name of the game.

5. *Put fear to work.* Why view fear as a negative when it can be a powerful motivator? Fear of forfeiting a home to the bank has launched more than one laid-off employee on the road to self-employment, and fear of failure pushes many entrepreneurs to work around the clock to get their businesses up and running. Remember that most successful entrepreneurs have been afraid at one time or another.

6. *Build a support network.* Talking to fellow entrepreneurs who have walked the same path you're about to embark on can help assuage your fears. Attend conferences, join associations, and talk with others who started as you did but who have moved on to the next step.

7. *Remember that you may have more assets than you realize.* For example, you might have money in the bank, friends in the industry, a supportive family, a good attitude, a great idea, an awesome partner, chutzpah, or a good education.

THE BOTTOM LINE

It is easy to get caught up in the romance of starting your own business. You need to avoid that trap. Before anything, you need to consider carefully both the pros and cons of entrepreneurship. Above all, starting a business is a calculated risk. Be sure to pick a business that you love, but also one you can afford and for which there is a need.

Resources You Can Use

Entrepreneur **Magazine**
<www.entrepreneur.com>

Inc. **Magazine**
<www.inc.com>

The National Association of the Self-Employed
800-232-NASE (800-232-6273)
PO Box 612067
DFW Airport
Dallas, TX 75261-2067
<www.nase.org>

The Service Corp of Retired Executives (SCORE)
800-634-0245
<www.score.org>

U.S. Chamber of Commerce
202-659-6000
1615 H Street, NW
Washington, DC 20062

The United States Small Business Administration
800-UASK-SBA (800-827-5722)
409 3rd Street, SW
Washington, DC 20416

2

The Home-Based Business Advantage

Don't make the mistake of already deciding that yours is not going to be a home-based business. The important thing to understand is that there are two types of home-based businesses, and yours might fall into either category.

The first category includes businesses that start at home and remain home-based. Many people start their business at home because it is an easy, convenient, and inexpensive option. And for these reasons, they intend to keep their business there.

But many people start their business out of their home with the idea of moving it out as soon as it is feasible. These folks understand that in the early, critical, start-up phase of their business, money is vital and starting from home affords them the luxury of spending their capital on needs other than rent, which is smart thinking.

It may not be surprising then that many businesses you know started out as a home-based business, such as:

- Disney
- Amazon.com
- Microsoft
- Xerox
- L.L. Bean
- Apple

Success leaves clues. These are some of the best businesses of all time. One thing they share is an understanding that a small, home-based business can turn into a big business. By saving their money and utilizing resources already available in their homes, the entrepreneurs who started these businesses were able to turn their attention, efforts, and capital toward their businesses. It's a valuable model to follow.

■ Real Life Example

In the 1950s, Bette Naismith was a single mom who worked as a bank secretary. Although she was not a great typist, she did happen to be a very good artist. So every year, the bank had her paint the Christmas scene for the bank's windows.

One year, she made a mistake while painting the holiday scene and just painted right over it, as artists are wont to do. She thought to herself, "I wish I could do that when I was typing." Her big idea came when she realized that she could.

She snuck some tempera paint into work and began to paint over her typos. She soon realized that this was a great product that she could sell to other secretaries. Working out of her house at night after she got home from work, Ms. Naismith began to experiment with different permutations of paint. By setting up her business at home, Bette Naismith was able to start the Liquid Paper Corporation, and revolutionize the office supply industry in the process.

The Home-Based Business Revolution

If you decide to start a business from home, you are not alone. More than ever, working from home has become an accepted method of conducting business. While more "traditional" home businesses such as mail order remain as strong as ever, professionals such as lawyers and architects are also moving home as well.

Indeed, working from home is now easier, and far more accepted, than ever before. It is estimated that roughly one million new home-based businesses are started every year. The number of home-based businesses in the

United States ranges from 15 million to 40 million, depending on who is doing the counting, and what they are counting.

Whatever the actual number, the fact is that home-based businesses can be very profitable. *Entrepreneur* magazine estimates that almost $500 billion is generated each year by home-based businesses. In a recent survey, the Small Business Administration (SBA) discovered that almost 25 percent of all home-based businesses had a yearly gross income between $100,000 and $500,000. If present trends continue, within ten years, one out of every three households will have someone working from home.

Whereas working from home used to be kept a secret, today there is a certain cache to working from home. It's hip. But there is usually no need to

■ Real Life Example

One day in the spring of 1994, Jeff Bezos was sitting at the computer in his 39th-floor office in midtown Manhattan, looking at something very few people had even seen—the Internet. Bezos happened upon a Web site that said that the Internet was growing at a rate of 2,300 percent *a year*. As Bezos later told *Time* magazine, "It was a wake-up call. I started thinking, OK, what kind of business opportunity might there be here?" Bezos knew that whatever he created had to be unique; offering something people couldn't get elsewhere. "Unless you could create something with a huge value proposition for the customer, it would be easier for them to do it the old way," Bezos told *Time* in 1999.

That is what finally led Bezos to books. He figured that selling books online would in fact be unique because online he could offer *every* book available. There were no giant mail-order book catalogs because such a catalog would have to list millions of books to be complete. Only on the Internet could Bezos offer every book.

So, Jeff Bezos quit his job, and set out with his wife MacKenzie for Seattle. Why Seattle? Because the city had two huge book distributors and plenty of computer experts he could hire. As MacKenzie drove them across the country, Jeff wrote his business plan on his laptop.

When they arrived in Seattle, Jeff and MacKenzie rented a two-bedroom home in Bellevue, a suburb of Seattle. It was there that they started their company. Converting the garage into a workspace, Amazon.com was born.

tell anyone that you work from home because the new entrepreneurial economy and its attendant information age has made it practically impossible to tell where someone works. Between fax machines, PCs, cell phones, personal digital assistants (PDAs), e-mail, and call waiting, anyone can be an executive in his bathrobe if he so chooses, and no one is the wiser.

This is good news for the would-be entrepreneur, because one of the advantages of setting up shop at home is that it drastically cuts down on overhead. This in turn makes it much more affordable and possible to start a business, and increases the potential for success.

Maybe your dream is to be a multimillionaire. That's fine. But so too is a dream to create a business that makes enough money to allow you to stay home, play with the kids when they get home from school, and shoot a round of golf on Friday afternoons. That's fine too. That you are the boss and can do what you want is one of the best things about starting your own home-based business. Doing what you want—that's the whole idea.

Risks and Rewards of Working from Home

Working from home, either necessary or by design, is not always an easy thing to do. There are definite distractions and other issues to contend with that one doesn't face when working in an outside office. But by the same token, there are benefits that other locales do not offer.

First the bad news. Working from home can be challenging. There are three common problems of which to be wary.

1. It's Easy to Get Distracted

One of the best things about working outside the house is that it forces you to give work the attention and rigor it deserves. When you go to work every day to an office full of people dressed well, who are (theoretically) committed to achieving the same goal, it forces you to take work seriously.

That is simply not true when you work for yourself at home. If you want to sleep in, you can. There is no one to report to but you. If you want to work in your pajamas, you can. It's pretty easy to find yourself watching too much TV, or wandering into the kitchen too often, or playing one round of golf too many. It's very easy to goof off when you work alone at home.

Another problem is that some people find it difficult to distinguish their personal life from their business life when they work at home. Just as it's easy to get swept up in the novelty of working from home and goof off too much, it also is easy to work too much. Workaholics need self-discipline too, lest they find themselves working at all hours of the day and night, letting their personal lives become nonexistent.

The bottom line is that if you are going to be a successful home-based businessperson, you need to have or learn some self-discipline.

2. It's Easy to Feel Alone

If it is easy to get distracted working from home, it is equally easy to feel isolated. Another good thing about going to a regular office every day is the social aspect of work. Work is a great place to meet people, exchange ideas, share a joke, and interact with other people.

You will be giving that up when you open your own home-based business. While it is certainly true that you may take on employees down the road, at the beginning of your venture, you are likely to be working alone. And at the start is when loneliness is most likely to crop up. One way that some home-based entrepreneurs handle this is by making sure to schedule meetings and business lunches with associates outside of the home, to maintain that social aspect of work.

Others experience the opposite feeling. Instead of feeling alone, they feel as if they lack privacy. Working at home allows your spouse, your kids, and any visitors to your home access to your workspace and your business. Having a separate office that everyone respects is a key element to successfully operating a home-based enterprise.

> Post your business hours on the door of your home office. People will be much less inclined to poke in when they know that you take your work schedule seriously.

3. You May Not Be Taken Seriously

It used to be that working from home was a bit of an oddity and the person who did so was considered an iconoclast at best. Things have certainly changed. With so many people working from home these days, it is far more acceptable and understood.

Nevertheless, SBA studies indicate that roughly 25 percent of home-based businesspeople still feel that they are not taken as seriously as their office-building–bound brethren. That is, customers, clients, business associates, former coworkers, and even family members may not appreciate that you are as professional as anyone working from a "normal" office. This perception is best dealt with by creating a professional image and a professional workspace, and doing top-notch work.

■ Real Life Example

Lillian Vernon was born in Leipzig, Germany, and escaped to New York with her family during World War II. Newly married and pregnant in 1951, Ms. Vernon used the $2,000 that she received as wedding gift money and started a mail order business in an effort to help pay household bills.

Her office was the kitchen table in their apartment. Ms. Vernon placed a sixth-of-a-page ad for personalized handbags and belts in *Seventeen* magazine and waited. The ad was a huge hit, bringing in more than $32,000 in orders. With success like that, the Lillian Vernon Company outgrew her home office in three short years.

Today, Lillian Vernon has sales of over $287.1 million, introduces more than 3,000 new products, and accepts 4.4 million orders each year.

Despite these three problems, the rewards of working from home are numerous. From a practical standpoint, succeeding in business is more likely with a home-based business than an outside business because it is much less expensive to run. Not only do you save on rent and related overhead, but there also is less mileage on your car, less need for expensive clothes, and substantial tax deductions available. Thus, your gross profit margin is greater than in a "regular" business. This is borne out by a 1999 SBA study that found that home-based businesses fail at a lower rate than conventional businesses.

Second, on a personal level, people who work at home tend to be a fairly happy lot. A survey conducted by *Prevention* magazine found that people who work at home say that they eat healthier, have more free time, exercise more often, and have a better sex life than when they were employees. In comparison, 45 percent of regular employees worry about their job, and 49 percent find their job to be very stressful, according to the *Prevention* study. People who work at home report that they have more time to spend with family members, also upping the happiness quotient.

That last point is important. Many people love working from home because it keeps them closer to the family. That hour or more that you commute every day is reduced to a 30-second walk, and the time saved can be spent as you wish, with whom you wish.

> "Millions have found their productivity actually increases when they work nearer the people they are really working for—their families."
> —President George Herbert Walker Bush.

Parents of young children also appreciate the chance to create a work schedule that allows them to be home and free when the kids are home from school. You can make your own schedule and work when it works for you, which may not necessarily be nine to five. Indeed, one of the greatest things about working from home is the ability to work at odd hours. You may decide that your hours should be from 7:00 AM to noon, and then again from 3:00 PM to 6:00 PM, or from 6:00 AM to 2:00 PM. Making work work for you is what this is all about.

Setting Up Shop at Home

To make working from home work for you, it is critical that you set up your home office properly. Setting it up takes some thought and careful planning. Sure, choosing where you'll spend the majority of your day, arranging furniture and supplies, and decorating your walls should be enjoyable, but there is a bit more to the logistics of choosing a home office than putting up pictures.

First, you need to pick the right room. It may be that only one room is available, but if you do have a choice, remember that you can never have too much space. The number one complaint among home businesspeople is not having enough space.

✎ Home Office Space Requirements Checklist

☐ **Working.** At a minimum, you need room for a desk, chair, computer, phone, other supplies.

☐ **Storage.** You will need a file cabinet and room for boxes and other storage goods.

☐ **Books and supplies.** You will need space for bookshelves.

☐ **Grunge work.** You will need space for assembling materials, stuffing envelopes, and the like.

☐ **Conference space.** If you will be meeting with clients, you will need room for chairs or a couch and a table.

☐ **Other.** Do you need space for employees? What about for specialized goods, a waiting area for clients, or production facilities?

You really need to have a separate room for your business. Not only is having space to yourself critical, but if you want to claim the home office tax deduction, you need a specific room for business only (see Chapter 12). By having a room dedicated to work only, you are sending a signal to yourself and those around you that even though you are at home this is about work. It forces everyone to take your venture more seriously. You can cordon off space in a large room using dividers if you have to, but avoid it if you can.

If you want a special room for your office and do not have one, consider converting a room for the purpose. An attic, basement, garage, or patio can be turned into a great workspace, and it need not cost a fortune. Some carpet, track lighting, and a new window can go a long way to making unused space very useful.

You also need to consider that you will require a place where you can work peacefully. Barking dogs, construction, and kids playing in the street can drive you to distraction. As such, insulating your new office may be worth the cost. Wall-to-wall carpeting is great for reducing sound, but even an area rug will help as long as you spring for good padding. Other sound-reduction tools include weather-stripping, double-glazed windows, and solid doors.

✎ **Home Office Infrastructure Requirements Checklist**

☐ **Electrical wiring.** It's usually worth the money to install extra outlets. If you do, consider installing them above desk level. If your office is going to be relatively equipment-heavy, consider placing those electrical outlets on a separate circuit breaker.

☐ **Phone lines.** You should have at least two phone lines, one for the phone and one for faxes. Make sure your phone jacks are close to electrical outlets to support equipment that requires both.

☐ **Internet.** Any home-based business starting today will need to get wired for high-speed Internet access. DSL lines eliminate the need for dialing, are up to 50 times faster than dial-up, and can accommodate multiple users on one connection. DSL is available through many different providers that can be found in your phone book or on the Net. Similarly, cable Internet access employs cable technology to provide high-speed access using your area's cable TV infrastructure. Your local cable company usually provides this service.

☐ **Ventilation.** In a forced-air system, there is usually a vent on the floor and one on the ceiling. Do not put your equipment near them.

☐ **Lighting.** Try to use as much natural light as you can. Add in a mix of ambient lighting (ceiling fixtures) and task lighting (a desk lamp).

Design your workspace with you in the center. You should be able to perform multiple tasks within reasonable reach. If you purchase furniture, you might want flexible spaces and cubbyholes for various items and equipment. Here are some other tips on creating a workspace that works:

- Make your bookshelves only as deep as necessary. Unless you store a lot of three-ring binders or other large books, a depth of eight inches should work. This will leave more floor space.
- Use the tops of filing cabinets to hold peripherals such as a printer and scanner.
- If you are buying a new computer and are really squeezed for space, consider a laptop. They take up far less desk or table space than a full-

size PC and have the obvious advantage of being portable. The down-side is that typing on a laptop keyboard can be tiring; make sure you choose one that is big enough for you.

- Shelves, pencil sharpeners, telephones, and lights can all be affixed to the wall instead of taking up precious floor or desk space.

It is strongly recommended that you set up a separate phone line for your new business and that you buy a two-line phone. You may even need three phone lines in your home—one for personal use, one for business use, and a dedicated fax/modem line. There are several advantages to having a separate business line for your business calls.

First, it is more professional. It conveys a message that yours is a legitimate business. Your answering machine/voice mail won't be asking your customers to leave a message for your teenage daughter, as it would if you shared a phone line with the family. A separate phone line keeps your business and your personal life separate.

Moreover, a separate phone line may mean that you will get more business. By having your business phone be an actual business line, the phone company will be able to list you in the business section of the White Pages and you will be able to have an ad in the Yellow Pages. It also means that you will get more done. Having one single line for home, business, computer, and fax simply makes no sense in this day and age.

Equipping a home office is not an inexpensive proposition. A desk, chair, and computer are, unfortunately, just the beginning.

The important thing to remember is that you will be spending a lot of time in this space, so make sure it reflects your temperament. The office items you buy and how you arrange them can make a world of difference in your productivity.

✎ **Home Office Equipment Requirements Checklist**

☐ **Desk.** You need a desk large enough for what you will be doing, but keep in mind that a huge desk can overpower a small room. In fact, a desk need not be big to be good, and plenty of compact computer desks are avaialble today. How much will you spend on a desk? It will run you anywhere from $200 to $2,000, depending upon your needs and budget.

☐ **Chair.** Usually, your chair is more important than your desk. If you will be sitting a lot, your chair is essential. Get a good one. A good ergonomic chair should cradle your back, encourage good posture, and allow for height, back, and arm adjustments. How much will you spend? Expect to spend at least $200 and easily more than $500 for an excellent chair.

☐ **Computer.** Don't skimp here. A cheap computer will be out of date in a year or two.

☐ **Copier/printer/scanner/fax machine.** These days, it is easy and affordable to buy one machine that handles all of these duties.

☐ **Two-line phone.** Preferably, you want a phone with a display that tells you who is calling on the other line.

☐ **Answering machine or answering service.** Answering services are not inexpensive. They can easily cost several hundred dollars a month, but may be worth it if yours is a business that requires a professional image.

☐ **File cabinet.** You can skimp here. Buy used.

☐ **Bookshelves.** Again, this is something you can buy used, although an attractive pressboard bookcase can be found at office supply stores for around $100.

☐ **Cell phone or pager.** Not everyone needs your cell phone or pager number.

> ### THE BOTTOM LINE
>
> Starting a business from home can be one of the best decisions you make. By drastically reducing your overhead, you correspondingly increase your chances of success. The important thing is to treat a home-business as you would any other business. When you act like a professional, no matter where your office is located, you will be treated as one.

Resources You Can Use

American Association of Home-Based Businesses
PO Box 10023
Rockville, MD 20849
<www.aahbb.org>

American Home Business Association
800-664-2422
4505 South Wasatch Boulevard, #140
Salt Lake City, UT 84124
<www.homebusiness.com>

HOMEBusiness Journal
315-865-4100
9584 Main Street
Holland Patent, NY 13354
<www.homebizjour.com>

***Home Business* Magazine**
949-462-0224
25211 Longwood Lane
Lake Forest, CA 92630

Buying Franchises and Other Businesses

One of the best ways to start a new business, if you do it right, is to buy a franchise or other established business. While people typically think of McDonald's, KFC, Dunkin' Donuts, or Baskin Robbins when they think of franchises, the fact is that franchises come in almost every industry. The same is true for an already established business. They can be found for sale in every industry and take a lot of the risk out of the entrepreneurship equation.

Franchises

Franchising is a method of distributing services or products. With a franchise system, the *franchisor* (the company selling the franchise) offers its trademark and business system to the buyer, or *franchisee*, who pays a fee for the right to do business under the franchisor's name using the franchisor's methods. The franchisee is given instructions on how to run the business as the franchisor does using the franchisor's name and the franchisor supports the franchisee with expertise, training, advertising, and a proven system.

Buying into a proven system is important. The franchises that work best are those where the franchisor has worked out the kinks and translated its business into a systematic procedure that the franchisee follows. Do what the franchisor did, and you should get the results that it got; that's the idea. As franchisors are wont to say, when you buy a franchise, you are in business for yourself but not by yourself.

The reason that a franchise can be a smart business decision is that in the right franchise system, the franchisor has already made the mistakes so you don't have to. Franchising should reduce your risk. You need not reinvent the wheel. In exchange for its expertise, training, and help, however, you will be required to give up some independence and do things the franchisor's way.

Are You Cut Out to Be a Franchisee?

In 1997, the *Franchise Times* conducted a survey of the "average franchisee." What it discovered was that the typical franchisee is a 48-year-old man who owns 3.5 franchises, works 52 hours a week, and attended college. But if that does not describe you, don't worry.

Franchisees come in all shapes and sizes and from all walks of life. Franchisees are people who usually want a career change; people who may be fed up with corporate life and dream of owning their own business. While that's a start, there is more to being cut out for the franchise world than a strong desire. From the franchisor's point of view, a good franchisee should be:

- Someone with a strong work ethic, motivation, and enthusiasm
- A person who may not have all the necessary entrepreneurial skills; i.e., someone who needs what a good franchisor has to offer
- Someone who is open and willing to learn new things
- Someone with management experience
- A person with knowledge of the industry (Note: This is not usually necessary for a fast food franchise.)
- Someone who is a good salesperson (Maybe the most important trait of all.)

If you think that a franchise is for you, the next step is to thoroughly check out possible franchisors. Not all franchises are created equal. Some franchisors give a lot of support and training, others give little. Some are easy to work with, some are not. The important thing is that you do your homework and learn about the franchise before buying.

Quiz: Are You a Potential Franchisee?

To help you decide whether you have the necessary qualities to be a successful franchisee, take the following quiz. As you do, be totally honest with yourself; a franchise is a major commitment of time and money. Circle yes or no.

[Yes]   [No]   I do not have to make all decisions for myself. I am willing to let others make some too.

[Yes]   [No]   I could fill in for an absent busboy if needed.

[Yes]   [No]   I do not need a lot of supervision.

[Yes]   [No]   I am willing to put long hours into the business.

[Yes]   [No]   I am willing to do what the franchisor suggests, even if I don't agree.

[Yes]   [No]   I am highly organized.

[Yes]   [No]   I have at least 5 years of management or teaching experience.

[Yes]   [No]   I have hired and fired employees.

[Yes]   [No]   I have trained personnel.

[Yes]   [No]   I am a good salesperson.

[Yes]   [No]   I have sufficient capital to buy into the franchise of my choice. (This is critical.)

[Yes]   [No]   I am willing to take a risk with my money to make money.

[Yes]   [No]   My spouse and family support my choice to start a franchise.

[Yes]   [No]   I am a self-starter.

[Yes]   [No]   I am willing to be a follower.

If you answered at least ten of the questions in the affirmative, then it is likely you have what it takes to make a franchise work. While all of these traits are important, realize that you must be highly motivated, persistent, willing to listen to the franchisor, and sales-oriented to be a successful franchisee.

■ **Real Life Example**

Hector was interested in a restaurant franchise. Given that he had begun work as a busboy and had moved up the ranks to become a general manager of a restaurant chain, he decided that owning his own franchise would be the next step. Hector settled upon one very well-known chain and began to do his research.

He was surprised to discover that many of the franchisees he talked to were very displeased with the franchisor. They felt that the franchisor was hard to work with, didn't follow through, and seldom listened to their ideas. Hector was even more surprised when he became attracted to a much smaller, less famous restaurant franchise.

Both his instincts and homework told him that the smaller franchisor offered a better opportunity. He was right. Within ten years, the small chain had grown exponentially, and Hector was there, almost from the beginning. His advice and expertise were actually welcomed and sought out by the franchisor. Hector eventually owned 12 stores in the chain.

Finding the Right Franchise

With so many franchise systems from which to choose, the options can be dizzying. It is best to start with a global perspective. In the universe of franchising, which industries seem to match your interests? Narrow the choices down to a few industries in which you are most interested, and then analyze your geographic area to see if there is a market for that type of business.

Once you have decided which industry interests you most and seems to have growth potential in your area, contact all the franchise companies in that field and ask them for information. Any reputable company will be happy to send you information at no cost.

A great place to learn about all of your options is at a franchise trade show. This is a terrific way to gather a lot of preliminary information and survey the field in a short period of time, and you can find them in most good-sized cities. When attending a franchise trade show, keep a few thoughts in mind. First, remember the companies exhibiting at the show by no means make up all of the franchise opportunities available. Indeed, these events showcase only a small selection of the available franchise programs.

Second, when you do go, take full advantage of the information available. Pass by the sellers who are out of your price range or do not meet your personal goals. Be sure to dress conservatively when you go to the show, carry a briefcase, leave the kids at home, and take business cards if you have them. Show the representatives you meet that you are a serious prospect. Have a short list of questions ready to ask them:

- What is the total investment required?
- What is a franchisee's typical day like?
- Is financing available from the franchisor?
- What kind of support can you expect from the franchisor?
- What is its advertising plan?

Of course, you cannot rely solely on promotional materials to make your decision; you also need to do your own research. *The most important thing you can do is talk to current and former franchisees.* They can tell you what it is like to work with the franchisor, how much money you can really expect to make, and what to be on the lookout for.

It also can be very helpful to visit your library or go online to look up all the articles you can find about the franchisors you are considering. Is the company depicted favorably? Is it growing? Check with the consumer or franchise regulators in your state to see if there are any complaints lodged against the companies you are considering. Be sure to check with the Federal Trade Commission, the better business bureau, and your local chamber of commerce.

Analyzing the Costs

Obviously, one of the most important things you must consider when choosing a franchise is the cost involved. There are three fees associated with buying a franchise. The first is the *franchise fee*. This is the amount you will pay the franchisor for the right to use its system and trademark. In a well-known food franchise, these fees typically run between $15,000 and $50,000. The second fee is the *royalty payment*. This is an ongoing monthly fee paid to the franchisor. Usually, it runs between 3 and 6 percent of gross monthly sales.

The final fee is the largest—the *cost of buying the actual physical business*. There are many costs associated with this. These include:

- *Real estate fees.* You may need to pay for a real estate agent to help you find a location. You will also have to put down a security deposit and utility deposits.
- *Architecture fees.* You may need either an architect or a civil engineer to create plans to modify (or design) your location. A good franchisor may have a set of standard architecture plans that you can use.
- *Contractor fees.* This is a big-ticket item. It can include everything from landscaping to major construction overhauls.
- *Equipment and fixtures.* You may need to buy everything from tables, chairs, telephone systems, kitchen equipment, and display counters to computer systems, software, and cash registers.
- *Décor.* This will include things like signs, pictures, lights, and interior design.
- *Inventory.* Your opening inventory includes many things, such as ingredients, raw materials, product, paper goods, office supplies, and janitorial supplies.
- *Insurance.* You will need to buy workers' compensation insurance (required by law), as well as liability, property, auto, and other insurance.
- *Labor costs.* You will likely need to hire staff and managers, and may need to pay for training with the franchisor.
- *Professional fees.* You may need to hire a lawyer and an accountant before you open your doors.
- *Working capital.* This is the amount of money you will need to keep the business going until it begins to turn a consistent profit. You probably need to have at least six months' worth of working capital before planning your grand opening party.

Needless to say, you shouldn't underestimate these costs. Nothing is worse than spending a lot of money to start your new business but not budgeting enough to keep it going until it becomes a success.

So, how much do you need? Let's examine some of the costs of various franchises in order to get an idea:

- *McDonald's.* McDonald's estimates that new restaurant costs range from $455,000 to $768,500. Many things affect those costs: the size of the restaurant, the area of the country in which it will be located, inventory, equipment, signs, décor, and landscaping. In addition, at the time of opening, a franchise fee of $45,000 is paid to McDonald's

Corporation. You must have in liquid cash a minimum of $175,000 for a conventional purchase or $100,000 for a lease. The rest can be financed, although McDonald's itself does not finance franchises.

- *Subway.* Subway estimates that new restaurant costs range from $97,000 to $222,800. While the franchise fee is only $10,000, the real costs are in building the restaurant, which includes leasehold improvements, signs, equipment, etc. Subway requires that you also have funds to operate the business for three months, above and beyond any other capital requirements.
- *ServiceMaster.* ServiceMaster provides services to homeowners such as cleaning, janitorial, maintenance, and disaster restoration. The capital requirements for this franchise range from $10,200 to $52,000. The franchise fee (between $14,500 and $26,500) as well as the equipment purchase can be financed up to 80 percent.
- *Meineke Discount Mufflers.* Meineke's franchise fee is $25,000, and it requires that you have a minimum of $50,000 in cash. Financing is possible to qualified candidates.
- *Mail Boxes Etc.* MBE's capital requirements range from $125,862 to $195,882. The franchise fee is $29,950. MBE offers up to 40 percent financing for fixtures and equipment.

With thousands of franchise choices available, and costs that vary greatly, it is incumbent upon you to do your research and find a franchise system that fits both your personality and your pocketbook. It is out there.

Analyzing the Franchisor

As you go about this research, understand that successful franchisors have certain traits in common. Following are the traits that are most important. If you can find a franchisor that has these traits, you are headed in the right direction.

The Franchisor Supports the Franchisees

The best franchises are ones where the franchisor sees its relationship with the franchisees as a partnership. As Steve Reinemund, the former head of Pizza Hut, puts it, "Franchisees are only as successful as the parent company and the parent company is only as successful as the franchisees."

Not only do such exceptional franchisors offer plenty of communication, opportunities for growth within the company, and help during hard times, they also offer lots of advice and training. A good example of this is Dunkin' Donuts. To support new franchisees, it created Dunkin' Donuts University. There, franchisees and their personnel are invited to attend a six-week success program that teaches them everything from basic instructions on how to run the business to how to produce the products, deal with employees, and use equipment. It even offers advice on inventory control and accounting. Now that's support.

The Franchisor Advertises a Lot

Not all franchises are dependent on advertising, but so many are that this is an important distinction. You want a system that does not skimp on advertising and promotions because that is where your customers will come from. Dunkin' Donuts spends roughly $40 million a year on extensive advertising campaigns for TV and radio, and in newspapers across the country. Similarly, Pizza Hut spends about 7 percent of its gross sales on sales and marketing. That is the kind of advertising support you should be seeking.

The Franchisor Offers Uniformity, Tempered with Flexibility

One of the great strengths of franchising is that customers know what to expect when they walk into a well-known franchise. For example, that sort of uniformity is one of the main reasons people choose to eat at McDonald's.

But by the same token, you want to avoid a franchisor that is so strict that it does not allow for creativity and some independence. The good franchisors know that some of the best ideas come from franchisees that try something new. One reason for buying a franchise is that you want the freedom to be your own boss. Avoid the paternal franchisor.

> The Big Mac was introduced at McDonald's in 1968. It was the brainchild of Jim Delligatti, one of McDonald's first franchisees.

The Franchisor Is Committed to Customer Service

The great franchisors don't just give lip service to customer service, they teach it to everyone in the organization, and live it on a daily basis. That's critical, because if people are treated well at other outlets, that, in turn, gives your individual franchise a good name too. As the Pizza Hut chairman put it, "We are committed to more than just good service, we are committed to providing legendary service."

The Franchisor Changes with the Times

Tastes and values change. The last thing you want is to buy into a system that is stuck in the past, not realizing that its product or service needs to adapt to the times. The better franchise systems are constantly test marketing new ideas and new products in an effort to stay ahead of the competition.

Typically, a good franchisor will provide the following services on an ongoing basis:

- Local, regional, and national advertising, offering you related programs and materials
- Field support
- Updates to the operating manual and ongoing related training for you and your management team
- Some sort of advisory council
- Research and development of new products, services, and system enhancements
- Communication support—either an intranet, a members-only Web site, monthly newsletters, or some other method to keep you up to date

If the franchisor you are considering does not offer these sorts of things, it would behoove you to think twice.

Meet the Franchisor

After narrowing your choices, it is time to sit down with the franchisor and get all of your questions answered.

■ Real Life Example

What kind of training do various franchisors offer? Here's a sampling.

Alphagraphics. Alphagraphics provides four weeks new franchisee training, one week in-store training, and advanced franchisee training; a toll-free technical support hotline; marketing and advertising programs including automated direct mail programs and newspaper and radio ads; ongoing training includes conferences and store visits by field reps.

Martinizing Dry Cleaning. Martinizing Dry Cleaning provides comprehensive managerial and technical training in the classroom as well as at franchisee's store; equipment shakedown and ongoing service hotline; a grand opening marketing package, and ongoing local store and marketwide promotional programs; field and operations assistance; ongoing support staff that is only a toll-free call away.

Fastsigns. Fastsigns provides initial site selection and finance assistance; four-week new owner training program; two-week on-site support during store opening; a grand opening marketing campaign; ongoing support includes marketing, operational, technical, and business management training as well as a fully integrated Internet system.

Petland. Petland provides a five-week training academy, which includes three weeks of on-site training prior to and following the grand opening; video and audio tapes backed up by operations manuals as resources for ongoing, in-store training; field operations managers to review monthly financial performance and provide consultations.

Tinderbox. Tinderbox provides complete turnkey, start-up assistance, which includes location, site selection negotiations, demographics, store layout, classroom training, on-site support operations manual, proprietary computerized operating system, and continuing operational support.

✎ Checklist of Franchisor Questions

- ☐ How much will the entire initial costs be, and what do they cover?
- ☐ How much will the franchise and royalty fees be?
- ☐ Will I be required to purchase land or can I lease? If I do lease, do you help me with the negotiations?
- ☐ What kind of building or construction costs will there be?
- ☐ What kind of equipment is required? What will it cost?
- ☐ What kind of initial training will I receive? What about ongoing training?
- ☐ Who supplies the starting inventory and what does it cost?
- ☐ What kind of promotional fees will I be expected to pay?
- ☐ Is there a fee for cooperative advertising? If so, how much is it?
- ☐ What kind of insurance will I be required to get?
- ☐ Will I be able to purchase supplies from you? If so, are the prices competitive with other suppliers?
- ☐ What sort of restrictions will I have with regard to competition with other franchisees?
- ☐ What are the terms regarding renewal rights and the sale of the franchise?

The important thing is that you get a very clear picture of the cost of purchasing the franchise—both start-up and ongoing costs. Once you have gathered all of this information, you will be able to make an informed decision. Carefully examine everything with your attorney, accountant, or business advisor. You want to be sure that every item of importance is addressed in the franchise contract.

Location, Location, Location

Not all franchises need to pick a dynamite location. For example, janitorial services, direct mail companies, or lawn care services really don't need to worry about their location because drop-in business is not their business model. But a restaurant needs a good location. Typically, if you are looking at a retail establishment, location usually is a priority.

The first thing to do is speak with the potential franchisor. One of the best aspects of buying into a good franchise operation is that you should get plenty of advice and help from the franchisor. Start there and see what it says. The franchisor will know what you should look for, what works best, and what locations are available in your area. In fact, in some cases, site location may not even be up to you; the franchisor may make this decision. You need to find out who chooses your location. If it is you, you want to make sure that the franchisor will be helping you in the site selection process.

Additionally, you need to find out about territorial exclusivity. Does the franchisor offer this and, if so, what is the size of the territory? Territorial exclusivity has been the subject of many lawsuits between franchisees and franchisors, so make sure that you really understand this issue and have any agreements put in writing.

As always, one of the best ways to know what to expect from a franchisor on this or any subject is to talk to the current franchisees. They will tell you if the franchisor plays fair, if territorial limits are respected, and if site location analysis is accurate.

Area Development

A topic related to location is area development. Area development allows you to open more than one franchise in a certain locale. If, for example, you want to open eight auto body repair shops, you can go to the franchisor and buy the rights to your area en masse. This allows you to monopolize the market and excludes challengers under the same franchise umbrella from competing with you. The key things to consider regarding area development are

- picking a franchise system that is not yet developed in the area, and
- getting the franchisor to grant you market exclusivity.

How Much Money Can You Reasonably Expect to Make?

All of this research begs the question: How much can you really make buying a franchise? The early days of franchise sales in the United States were marked with many instances of abuse in which misleading earnings claims were used to sell franchises. In 1979, in an effort to try to stop these practices, Congress authorized the Federal Trade Commission (FTC) to regulate the franchise industry. While the current FTC rules do not forbid a franchise company from supplying information about earnings, they do have tough rules on how this information can be given to a prospective franchisee.

Basically, if a franchise does want to provide this information, it must put it in its disclosure document, called the Uniform Franchise Offering Circular (UFOC, see sidebar and next section). Most franchisors opt not to disclose this information. Why? There are three reasons. First, it is not so easy to put together an accurate, reflective, earnings estimate. Second, the results may

An important legal protection for the person planning to buy a franchise is the Federal Trade Commission's Franchise Rule, put into effect October 21, 1979. The rule requires covered franchisors to supply a full disclosure of the information a prospective franchisee needs in order to make a rational decision about whether to invest in that particular franchise.

There are several requirements mandated by the Franchise Rule. First, the disclosure must take place at the first personal contact where the subject of buying a franchise is discussed and at least ten business days prior to signing any contract with the franchisee or accepting any money. This is designed to allow the potential franchisee a "cooling-off" period. What this means is that a franchisor, franchise broker, or anyone else representing franchises for sale must present a disclosure document, called the Uniform Franchise Offering Circular (UFOC), to the potential franchisee long before any money is exchanged. The UFOC contains extensive information about the franchise.

Furthermore, the Franchise Rule mandates that the potential franchisee must be provided with completed contracts covering all material points at least five days prior to the actual date of signing the contract.

simply not be attractive enough to entice new franchisees to join. Third, once it's in writing, the estimates may be seen as a benchmark, and if a franchisee fails to hit that mark, they just might sue the franchisor for making false promises. Because they don't want to get sued, many franchisors simply refuse to divulge this critical information.

When a franchise does not provide an earnings claim in its UFOC, it is still possible to get this information. The best way to find out how much money you can make is by asking existing franchisees. Make sure to select enough franchisees to get a clear picture of the ranges for earnings within the franchise system.

A good rule of thumb is that you can earn 10 to 15 percent on your money over time in a passive investment. Because most franchises require that you invest your time and efforts, as well as your money, you should expect a significantly higher return in order to justify the investment. You should look for earnings of at least 30 percent of your total investment on an annual basis to consider any franchise as having a reasonable return, and you should expect to reach this level, at the latest, by the third year of operation of the business.

Analyzing the UFOC

The franchisor is obligated under law to provide you with the UFOC at your first face-to-face meeting. The UFOC, though often written in legal gobbledygook, is nevertheless a wealth of information. There are 23 standard items in the document. The key areas you should concentrate on are as follows:

- *Item 2* describes the business background of the officers, directors, and managers of the franchisor. Scan these summaries to get an idea of their experience. You definitely want to make sure that they know what they are doing.
- *Item 3* summarizes the litigation background of the franchisor and the people listed in Item 2. If they have been sued a lot, a red flag should go up. If there have been actions taken by state or federal enforcement agencies against the company or its officers, or if private lawsuits have been filed against the franchisor in the past ten years, they are summarized in this section. Look especially for cases where franchisees have sued the company.
- *Item 4* lists any bankruptcies in the backgrounds of either the company or the people listed in Item 2.

- *Items 5 and 6* summarize the initial franchise fees and any ongoing royalty fees and other charges franchisees must pay. Go over these numbers with your accountant.
- *Item 7* presents the franchisor's estimate of the typical total investment by the franchisee. You will need this information when you prepare your business plan or if you will be seeking financing for the franchise. Again, go over this with your accountant.
- *Item 8* discloses the restrictions placed on your ability as a franchisee to purchase supplies and products. You need to investigate whether other franchisees think these products are fairly priced. Because supply arrangements are a vital aspect of running a business, make sure their system works well.
- *Item 10* discusses financing. Many franchisors either provide their own financing or make arrangements with banks or other lenders to assist franchisees. Even if there is no mention of special financing arrangements in this item, ask the franchisor about them.
- *Item 11* is the longest section in the document and it is critical. It discusses the franchisor's obligations to the franchisee under the franchise agreement. It also describes required computer equipment purchases and initial training programs.
- *Item 12* explains your territorial rights. If the franchisor reserves the right in this item to distribute competing products or services through other channels of distribution, find out how the company intends to use that right.
- *Item 13* details your ability to use the franchisor's trademark—the company's name and logo.
- *Item 19* explains potential profits. This important section shows what kinds of sales or profits other franchise owners have made. Interestingly, the franchisor is not legally obliged to supply this information in this section, and many don't. If a franchisor does provide this information, it must also provide data to prove the claims if you so request it. If the franchisor supplies no profit information here, find out why. It may be because the franchisees don't make a lot of money, or it could simply be that earnings vary widely from one region to another, or from one franchisee to another. The important thing in this realm is to go beyond what the UFOC says and ask franchisees about their sales and profits. Most are happy to share their experiences.
- *Item 20* contains statistical information, such as how many new stores have opened over the past few years and how many franchisees have

recently left the system. This section also contains a list of the names, addresses, and telephone numbers of current franchisees and those who have left the system in the past year. That alone makes the UFOC worth its weight in gold.

Common Mistakes to Avoid

Once all of your questions have been satisfactorily answered, you have done your due diligence and have spoken with existing franchisees, and you understand where your store will be located, it is time to sign on the dotted line. But before you do, make sure you avoid potential pitfalls. Franchisees often buy into a franchise without a full understanding of just what it takes to succeed in their chosen business. That is one of several common mistakes that are easily avoidable. The following are the mistakes you want to avoid when buying a franchise.

Not reading, understanding, or asking questions about the UFOC. The Uniform Franchise Offering Circular is a big document, sometimes 75 pages long, but it is critical that you read and understand each item, 1 through 23. As you read the document, keep notes on those areas that are confusing. Don't assume the franchisor is responsible for one thing or another; if it's not spelled out in the UFOC, ask! List all of your concerns, and clarify which duties, obligations, and responsibilities belong to whom. Then, have your lawyer read the document and do the same thing. Finally, go over each issue, item by item, with the franchisor. Get everything that the franchisor promises and agrees to in writing and have it made part of the franchise agreement.

Not understanding or having an inaccurate understanding of the franchise agreement and other legal documents. You and your attorney must carefully review the franchise agreement, lease and real estate agreements, and all other contracts. Any promises that the franchisor made earlier must be made part of your contract to be legally binding.

Not analyzing the market properly. While the franchisor may help with site selection, it is nevertheless your responsibility to decide whether a particular location is promising. Is there sufficient traffic? What is the competition like? Are the competitors so strong that their market saturation may be hard for you to penetrate? You have to conduct sufficient research to make sure that there is a market for your service or product in your chosen location.

Not checking out failed franchises. Locate some franchises that closed, were sold, or have changed ownership to company-owned, and find out the reasons for the change. Contact the original owners and get their stories. If there is a common theme, the underlying problem may be something you want to avoid.

Not contacting enough current franchisees. The section of the UFOC on "Past, Current, and Future Franchisees" is a great starting point for locating franchisees to contact. It is very important to speak with them. Only they really know how the franchisor is to work with, how much money you can expect to make, what mistakes to avoid, and the like.

Other than the franchisees introduced to you by the franchisor, you should also survey other franchisees not listed in the disclosure document. Find out from them if the franchisor has a reputation for honesty and verify their experience with the accuracy of the UFOC.

Not meeting with the franchisor's key management personnel at their headquarters and the representative assigned to your territory. A sales representative can do such a good job that you may not bother meeting the other important personnel or traveling to the headquarters before signing the franchise agreement. Do not make this mistake. Meet everyone you can and ask all the questions you can. Verify the information provided by the sales representative. After the franchisor defines your territory, meet the field representative or district supervisor that will be working with you.

Not having enough working capital. Money is the lifeblood of your business. Make sure you have enough capital to cover every cost associated with the business, including all preopening costs, your family budget, and operating capital for the business to make it through the break-even point.

Buying a Business

As in the case of a franchise, a preexisting business can be a great option, *if* you do it right. The fact is, you need not be an innovator to be a successful entrepreneur. Many entrepreneurs are great turnaround artists. They have far more success recognizing an opportunity and capitalizing on an existing venture than starting their own business. While you really never know what will happen when you create a business, when you buy an existing business, you can do enough research to be fairly certain what to expect. As such, buying an ongoing concern is less risky than starting a brand-new business.

The key to a business purchase is to dig into the business's records and history. If the past is prologue, then knowing what has happened in the venture will tell you where it is headed. The main things to check out include location, profits and losses, and people.

Location

How long has the business been in that location? It is a good sign if the store has been operating in the same place for many years. Conversely, if other businesses have failed in that location, you should be concerned. Some locations get a bad reputation in the neighborhood, and you should probably avoid those locations. You also want to be sure that the place is convenient for customers, has adequate traffic flow, is up to code, has adequate signage, and does not need a lot of remodeling. Finally, you need to see where your competition is in relation to the location.

Profits and Losses

You are buying a business presumably because you want an accurate idea of what your profit will be. To figure this out, you need to get from the proprietor the past five years' worth of audited balance sheets, income statements, and cash flow statements. Your accountant should review these. You need a copy of the lease and any other contracts for which you will be responsible. You need to get a list of assets and liabilities, receivables, and obligations. You need five years' worth of tax returns. Basically, you need all records as they relate to the business, and you need to spend time analyzing these records with your accountant.

People

You will be buying not only the business but also the staff. Review personnel files and meet with employees individually. Find out whether any have contracts that could prevent you from letting them go for any reason. You also need to speak with some of the business's customers. Discover what they think of the business, how they like it, and how long they have patronized it. That alone will tell you a lot.

Finally, make sure the owner is someone you can work with. He or she should disclose all financial, legal, personnel, and customer information. If information is refused, then there's a problem.

THE BOTTOM LINE

Buying into a good franchise or a successful business means that many of the bugs in the system have been worked out and many of the mistakes have already been made. Accordingly, buying a franchise or existing business is smart because, if done correctly, it can help reduce the risk inherent in entrepreneurship. The secret to doing so successfully is to do a lot of homework so that you will know exactly what it is you are getting.

Resources You Can Use

American Franchisee Association
312-431-0545
53 West Jackson Boulevard, Suite 205
Chicago, IL 60604
<www.franchisee.org>

Entrepreneur.com Franchise Zone
<www.entrepreneur.com/Franchise_Zone>

The Franchise Handbook
414-272-9977
c/o Enterprise Magazines, Inc.
1020 North Broadway, Suite 111
Milwaukee, WI 53202

The Franchise Times

651-631-4995

2500 Cleveland Avenue North, Suite D South

Roseville, MN 55113

<www.franchisetimes.com>

The International Franchise Association

202-628-8000

1350 New York Avenue, NW, Suite 900

Washington, DC 20005-4709

4

Preparation, Production, and Distribution

People go into business to sell products or to provide a service. That's it. It follows then that the very heart of your business will be your ability to produce those goods or services at reasonable prices so that you can make a profit when you sell them.

Planning for Your Service

Service businesses must provide their service, whatever it is, efficiently, quickly, affordably, and affably. It's a tall order. If you are opening a veterinary clinic, for example, your office has to set appointments that you will be able to keep on time, provide a bright and cheery atmosphere, offer valuable and affordable services, and have a staff that is friendly and knowledgeable.

If you think about it, that's essentially the same prescription for success for any service business. A carpet cleaning business, a law office, an auto repair shop, or a health club all must provide affordable and efficient services. How do you do that? The first step is systemization. You need to set up procedures and processes that will be followed every time for every customer or client.

Begin with your computer system. There is a lot of specialty software out there aimed at different sorts of businesses. You can bet that someone, somewhere, has created a program for a veterinary office that allows them to take appointments, track animals, and create bills. The vet needs to find that program just as you need to find the program for your service business. These programs are the first, critical step toward professionally producing your service.

■ Real Life Example

"When I opened my first law office, I wasn't sure what sort of law would become my 'specialty.' One day, shortly after I began, I received a phone call from an ad seller at my local newspaper. He had gotten my number from a listing of new business phone numbers.

The man asked me if I wanted to advertise in the paper's classified section, specifically, in the service directory. It sounded like a good idea to me, so I said yes. He asked me what my specialty was, and I told him that I wasn't sure. He then told me something that would change my life. 'If you want the phone to ring,' he said, 'you will put in an ad for bankruptcies.' I had done a few bankruptcies at the time, so I agreed; I wanted the phone to ring.

And he was right. Soon enough potential bankruptcy clients starting calling. My first bankruptcy took me 12 hours to prepare as I had to type in forms found in the back of a book. I soon bought a bankruptcy-preparation software program, and cut my time down to an hour. After a few years, I could pop one out in less than half an hour."

Beyond computers, training is essential to producing a winning service business. All employees have to be on the same page, with a common understanding of what is expected of them and where the business is headed. Most employees today want to do more than just put in their time and take home a paycheck. They want to feel they are part of something important; that their work makes a difference. Your job is to help them feel that way. Let them know your vision for the business and for them.

You might consider coming up with a mission statement for your business that you all agree on. Many small businesses have a mission statement prominently displayed in the office to which the employees often pay lip service. But great service businesses get their employees to actually buy into that mission and believe in it. When employees don't understand what the business is about, or if they are forced to heed some maxim on a plaque that they neither buy into nor believe is true, morale suffers.

Beyond having a shared mission, the smart entrepreneur will also be, like Ronald Reagan, a great communicator. Good communication could entail a quarterly "state of the company" report to employees, encouraging them to give suggestions or ask questions, or one-on-one meetings with employees devoted to career goals. This fosters a sense of teamwork, a major factor in developing a superior service business, according to a Department of Labor survey.

Take Starbucks, for example. Howard Schultz of Starbucks believes that teamwork is so critical to the company's success that employees (called "partners" in Starbucks-speak) spend several days after being hired learning how to be part of the Starbucks team and how to provide superior service. Schultz tells all new employees (about 500 a month), via video, how happy he is to have them on board. Even part-time workers repeatedly hear how much they are valued during the 24 hours of training they get in their first 80 hours of employment. Training is essential if you want your service to stand out.

The final thing you can do to create a great service business is properly reward your employees for providing superior service. Rewards can take many forms, but the most obvious are compensation, profit sharing, and benefits. Less evident rewards can also make a difference. A gift certificate, a luncheon to honor employees who have made outstanding contributions, or free T-shirts all help boost morale.

Creating a great place to work, one where people feel motivated, engaged, and part of a team with a purpose, can do a lot toward making your service business shine.

Your Product

Certainly not all businesses will be producing their own products. Retail stores are lined with products produced by others. And yet producing your own innovative product can also be one of the most lucrative businesses. Creating a product that speaks to people, fulfills a market need, and becomes a necessary and useful item is a rare sort of business home run that companies live for.

And yet there is no shortage of obstacles to creating the magic product. Whether it is finding the money to produce the product or convincing consumers that they need to have the latest cutting-edge gadget, turning innovative ideas into great products is no easy task. The first step in this process is determining if there is a market for the product.

Test Marketing

Every year, thousands of entrepreneurs face challenges similar to yours. Will their product sell? At what price? To whom will they be selling? Researching your market will answer these key questions for you. Before you invest a lot of time and money into producing your product, you need to sit

 Market Researching Your Product

Step 1: Begin with your potential customers. You need demographic data about them. The answers to the following sorts of questions will help you figure out to whom you will be selling your product:

- What is their age, gender, and marital status?

- Do you know their income level and occupation?

- Are they conservative or trendsetters?

- Do they have political, religious, or environmental beliefs that will influence their buying?

- Do they spend money freely and demand top quality, or do they shop for bargains?

Step 2: Meet with potential customers. Hire a market research firm or conduct the research yourself. Find out what they like and don't like about products similar to the one you will be producing. Devise a simple survey and give people a reason to fill it out. Find out what similar products they buy and what products they would like to see from you.

Step 3: Scope out the competition. Which products are similar to yours? How can they be improved? How can your product be made less expensive?

Step 4: Analyze the data.

down and look at your market to make certain you will be targeting the right buyers and offering products they want and can afford.

Market research is what Pete Meyers, founder of Pete's Beer (name changed by request) in Sacramento, California, did. When Meyers came up with a new product idea last year, he didn't hire big-name consultants to do market research. Instead, he tapped M.B.A. students at a local university business school. "My partner and I needed to know if retailers and consumers would be receptive to the product," Meyers says. Over four months, they gathered information, and the deeper the students dug, the better the idea looked. Meyers paid the school $2,500 for what he estimates was $100,000 worth of research and the students received an invaluable, real-world education.

Other options for inexpensive product research include:

- Interviewing prospective customers at shopping malls or other busy retail areas
- Conducting a telephone survey
- Asking your friends, neighbors, and colleagues what they think of your idea

Once you are convinced that you have a viable product, the final step before an all-out rollout of your product is to do some test marketing. Get your product into five or ten stores and see if it sells. Test different prices and displays to see what works best. After a successful test market run, it is time to mass-produce your product. The whole idea is to learn as much as you can about your new product before throwing a ton of money at it. Although all of this homework will take some time and cost some money, it's a lot better than producing on a hunch.

Producing Your Product

There are two ways to produce your product—either you can do it yourself or you can outsource it and have someone else produce it for you.

Producing Your Product Yourself

Producing your product begins with an analysis of what you will need to go from A to Z, and how much that will cost you. The first thing to consider is how many units you need to create every month. Creating 10,000 machine-made widgets and 10 handmade chairs are very different tasks. Once you have a good idea about what your production schedule is going to be, you can go about procuring the equipment and materials needed to create your product.

Make a list of what tools and machinery will be needed to produce the product. Which of these do you already have and which can you afford to buy? If you can't afford to buy the necessary equipment, consider leasing what you need.

As you go about setting up your production facility, make sure that you have enough room to expand should that (hopefully!) be necessary. Also keep in mind:

- Your facility needs to be safe for employees, and may have to meet safety regulations required by your city or state.
- Producing pollutants will require that you be able to dispose of them properly.
- A testing facility (such as Underwriters Laboratories) may be required to certify the safety or quality of your products.
- Bar codes may be required to sell your product in various stores.

The key thing to producing your own product for sale is that you can create it quickly, safely, and inexpensively without sacrificing quality. If you can't, then you need to hire someone to create the product for you.

Hiring Someone to Create Your Product

Tool and dye shops, machine shops, wholesale producers, artisans, seamstresses, plastic molders, and a host of other wholesale manufacturers are available for hire in most cities and they already have many of the tools necessary to produce your product.

The important thing is to find a manufacturer who will be able to affordably produce your product according to your specifications. Shop around. Prices and quality vary widely. Get samples and references and check up on the company. Find out how reliable they are and assess the level of quality of the goods they already produce. In some instances, hiring a production facility in another country may be the best, most affordable way to produce your product. An Internet search will produce a variety of manufacturers who may fit the bill.

Distribution

Finding a distribution channel for your product is critical. Entrepreneurs often take all the necessary steps—developing a great product, creating a prototype, patenting their ideas, and producing an initial batch of products—without considering the final step—how the product will be sold.

How important is this step? Consider that after Jeff Hawkins invented the PalmPilot, he had a very hard time getting his new product onto store shelves. His company finally decided to partner with (and eventually be bought out by) U.S. Robotics because that company had a distribution channel that Palm could tap that lead to it becoming a huge success.

But you need not go to such lengths to distribute your product. Here's a simple method you can use to get on store shelves. First, find a retailer who sells products similar to yours and ask from whom they purchase those products. Once you find out, contact that distributor, sales representative, or wholesaler and ask them what kind of deal they typically offer product manufacturers such as yourself. It is important to realize that both the distributor and the final retailer will want to mark up your product, so you have to price it accordingly from the outset. After you have spoken with one distributor, finding others should be easier. There may be dozens of wholesalers or distributors that distribute products similar to yours. Once you have spoken with a few, you will have a much clearer idea about which one may be best for you, as well as how to price your product properly to get it to market and begin generating some sales.

Product Innovation

Product innovation is one of the most sought after and talked about attributes in business. But all too often, innovation is more theory than practice because initiating and implementing an innovative product is rarely easy. It often takes a genius idea, total commitment, and plenty of money before the breakthrough product is accepted by consumers.

How then do you create a great product? Here are seven lessons for product innovators:

1. *Think of things that never existed and ask, "Why not?"* Bobby Kennedy's famous motto is an apt description of the first ingredient nec-

essary to create a great new product. Terrific products come from in-spired ideas. When George de Mestral took an annoying burr from his sock and placed it underneath his microscope, creating a break-through product like Velcro was the last thing on his mind. He spent the next ten years trying to duplicate artificially what nature made effortlessly.

2. *Tap the power of one.* The second lesson in product innovation is that one person can make a difference. Look at almost any product and you will invariably find that there was some man or woman be-hind it who was steadfastly committed to its success. Ed Lowe was nothing but a young, ambitious veteran with tons of unsold clay when he decided that he had an idea for a better cat litter. Crisscrossing the country in his old car, bartering his way into cat shows, and changing cat boxes one at a time is what it took for him to make Kitty Litter a success.

3. *Keep it simple, stupid.* No, no one is calling you dumb. Rather, the rule—keep it simple, stupid—and its acronym KISS are great ways to remember the third lesson of great products. If you are going to offer something new and improved, make sure that it is simple and does one or two things very well.

4. *First is best.* Getting your product to market first can often mean the difference between having a winner and being a loser. Post-it Notes were first. Tupperware was first. Pampers were first. Barbie was first.

5. *Try, try again.* The path of the innovator may not follow a straight line, grasshopper. Getting a product right often takes trial and error, followed by a few mistakes, a couple of bonehead moves, and only then, maybe, a home run. When Dr. Percy Spencer noticed that the chocolate bar in his pocket melted after standing near a magnetron tube, he realized that something unique had occurred. Yet it would take almost 20 years of trial and error before Raytheon could turn that into a microwave oven that could be used by the public.

6. *It's risky business.* Creating a great product and getting it out there often takes everything an entrepreneur has to offer. The financial risks involved, not to mention the emotional toll, are considerable in-deed. When two auto designers in California created a secret budget and dared their German superiors to take a risk on a car their bosses associated with Hitler, they were risking their careers. And when Volkswagen agreed to produce the New Beetle, it risked being per-

ceived as a backward-looking company. Great new products require risk; it is as simple as that.

7. *Synergy is necessary.* Synergy is a concept in which the whole is thought to be greater than the sum of its parts. For a product to succeed wildly, synergy is usually necessary. Take the PalmPilot, for instance. Although Jeff Hawkins is a brilliant engineer, he needed someone who could steer his genius toward business success. That person was Donna Dubinsky. Together, these two made a formidable team. Dubinsky needed Hawkins's mind, and Hawkins needed Dubinsky's business acumen. It was their yin and yang, forming a better whole, that allowed them to make the PalmPilot what it is.

If you are interested in learning more about product innovation, be sure to check out my book *The Big Idea: How Business Innovators Get Great Ideas to Market* (Dearborn Trade, 2001).

THE BOTTOM LINE

The ability to produce your product or service consistently and efficiently will determine to a great extent how successful your venture will be. It is critical that you test-market your idea before rolling it out, and remember that innovation is what really sets your business apart.

Resources You Can Use

Center for Innovation in Product Development
Building E60-275
Massachusetts Institute of Technology
617-253-3645
77 Massachusetts Avenue
Cambridge, MA 02139
<http://web.mit.edu/cipd/>

Product Development & Management Association
800-232-5241
17000 Commerce Parkway, Suite C
Mount Laurel, NJ 08054

Getting Started

In this section, you begin to put the first pieces of the successful business puzzle together. You learn how to plan properly and choose a great name and location. You also find out where the money to fund the business may be located.

5

Planning Your Business

The first four chapters of this book were intended to help you pick a business that you will love. That is, and will be, the "technical" part of your business: The florist will create bouquets, the interior designer will decorate homes.

For our purposes, it does not matter what the technical part of your business will be. The remainder of this book is a model of business success for any business of any kind; plop any technical job into this model, and the result will be business success.

So, for example, the florist, the interior designer, and you too will all need to pick a great name, find funding, create a great image, advertise, and grow. Those are the sorts of things that you will learn from here on out—a model for business success.

However, the biggest mistake you can make right now is to actually start that business. What you need to do instead is sit back, take a breath, and think. Your idea for that new business may be a winner, but it may not. What you need to do now is analyze your idea, analyze the industry, make sure others think you have a great idea, and make sure there is a market for your product or service. That is the first step in the business success model. A hunch will simply not do. You need facts to back up your plan.

Of course, the thought of quitting your job, taking a risk, and making some big bucks is pretty darn exciting; that's the whole idea. Starting a business is a grand adventure. But just like any adventure, before you ship off you want to have a pretty good idea of where you are going, how you will get there, and what you will do once you are there. So beginning in this chapter and continuing for the next few chapters, I want to help you put together a solid foundation for your business (ad)venture. This foundation consists of conducting market research, drafting a business plan, structuring the business, and, finally, securing your financing. Once you have done all this, then you can start your business.

Slow Down There, Cowboy!

There are many businesses that begin and fly by the seat of their pants, but yours shouldn't be one of them. It is easy to get so excited about a new business that you want to jump in without putting the foundation in place. But if you do get started without thinking through what you are going to do, how you are going to do it, how you will finance it, and how you will make money doing it, your chances of success are much lower than if you had considered these things.

Market research is critical. Before you put your hard-earned money and precious time into an untried business concept, a little effort up front will tell you if your idea makes sense. And you need to be prepared to go in a different direction if your research indicates that it is necessary. Facts trump hunches.

Is Your Idea Feasible?

Before you jump in, indeed before you do anything, you first must figure out if there is a market for your proposed business. The first law of business is (or at least should be): You must fulfill a market need. If there is no one around who wants or is willing to pay for your proposed product or service, your business will fail; it is as simple as that. So before you name the business, or get a business license, or take out an advance on your credit card, you need to do some market research.

Is there a market for a woman-oriented bookstore in your neighborhood? Market research will help you find out. Analyzing the market and industry is a way to gather facts about potential customers and determine the demand for your product or service. The more information you gather, the greater your chances of capturing a segment of the market. That is why you

■ Real Life Example

In the late 1970s, board games were old news. Monopoly was 50 years old, and Scrabble was even older. So, when Chris Haney and Scott Abbot got together to play a board game one night, they chose one of the very few available—Scrabble. As they pulled out Chris's Scrabble game, the two friends discovered that some of the tiles were missing. As they went out to buy another Scrabble game, Chris thought: This was the sixth game of Scrabble he'd bought in his life. The two friends decided then and there to start a business and invent a board game.

To say they were novices would be generous; they knew next to nothing about business or toys. They were journalists. Yet in their case, ignorance was not such a bad thing because they were aware of what they didn't know. They did what you are being coached to do—they began to research and analyze their industry. In January 1980, armed with an expired press pass and a camera without any film, the two buddies visited the Canadian Toy and Decoration Fair in Montreal posing as reporter and photographer. There, they pumped toy manufacturers for information about the strategies of marketing a game and, according to Scott, collected about $10,000 worth of information in one afternoon.

Their research convinced them that they were on to something—even though there had been few new board games invented over the previous half century, there was nevertheless a market for their new product and business. And they were right. After almost going broke in the process, the two friends sold more than 20 million copies of Trivial Pursuit within three years.

need to know your potential market before investing your time and money in any business venture. You don't want to waste time or money on a bad idea.

In essence, you must ask yourself whether anyone wants or needs your proposed business. In addition, it is equally important to research your potential competition, and the industry in general, so you can have a good idea about what you are getting into. By figuring out your potential market, your likely competition, and how you will stand out from the crowd, you greatly increase your chances of success.

✎ Understanding Your Market

These questions will help you collect your thoughts and begin to flesh out your idea.

1. Whom are your customers going to be? _____

2. Are there enough customers to support your business? _____

3. What is it that they need? _____

4. How are these needs not being serviced by existing businesses? _____

5. How is it that you will service those needs?_____

6. Who is the competition? _____

7. What are they doing right and wrong? _____

8. How will your business be different than your competitors'? _____

9. Why would customers leave your competitor and come to you?_____

10. What are the trends in your industry? _____

There are several methods you can use to gather the market information you need. The following descriptions of some of these direct and secondary methods will help you decide which methods may be best for you.

Direct Research

These methods are the most expensive, but they will give you the best results. Conducting direct research, either yourself or through a firm you hire, surveys the public regarding your proposed business.

There are basically three ways to conduct this research: on the phone, through direct mail, or in personal interviews.

Telemarketing and phone research. Telephone research is the least expensive of these methods, costing about one-third less than personal interviews. They also allow you to cover a broad geographic area.

Here are some tips to follow when using this technique:

- Tell the interviewee up front how important his or her response is and that the interview will be short (between five and ten minutes).
- Avoid pauses as respondent interest drops.
- Keep the questions short and interesting.
- Make the survey answer options consistent.

Good interviewers can survey up to seven people an hour (however, speed for speed's sake is not the goal of any of these surveys), but five to six per hour is more typical. You would like to get over 250 interviews to have a good sample.

The costs associated with this method include the fee for the telemarketer, phone charges, preparation of the questionnaire, and the analysis of the results. Costs can be lowered by calling during certain hours.

Direct mail. Direct mail questionnaires can be inexpensive if you send out enough to take advantage of bulk mail prices, but the response rates are usually less than 5 percent. To increase your response rate, try these ideas:

- Include a nice letter that explains what you are looking for and why.
- Keep your questions short.
- Limit the length of the questionnaire to two pages.
- Address the letter to a person, not "occupant."
- Address the letters by hand (tiring yes, but also effective).
- Include a self-addressed, stamped return envelope.

The main costs of this method relate to printing the cover letter and questionnaire, envelopes, postage, and the ensuing analysis.

Personal interviews. There are two main types of personal interviews, individual and group. Group interviews are good because you get many responses at once. They give insight into buying preferences and purchasing decisions. But they also are expensive because participants usually want to be paid for their time. One-on-one interviews either use a script to get responses to specific inquiries or are more open-ended, allowing for any response.

Costs for personal interviews include the fees paid to participants and interviewers, renting the facility, the printing of any questionnaires, and analysis.

If primary research is too expensive for you, then you need to turn to the secondary research methods discussed below. But before you do, it doesn't hurt to simply go out and speak with some business owners on your own. Go to a town other than your own (so that you aren't viewed as the competition), find a business similar to the one you want to start, and ask the owner about the business. Find out who his customers are, what they like and dislike, and what the competition is doing. By doing this several times, you will learn much about your potential business.

Secondary Research

There are many organizations and sources out there from which you can gather plenty of information that will help you make some informed decisions about your potential business. Government departments, public libraries, your local chamber of commerce, business departments at universities, and the Small Business Administration all have information that could help you.

Particularly helpful tools are trade organizations and associations. Almost every industry has a trade association and a trade publication associated with it. If anyone will know your potential industry, it is them. Most trade associations have regional chapters that usually are very helpful.

You can't overlook the greatest research tool invented in the past 100 years—the Internet. The Net is loaded with almost more information than you need regarding every business imaginable.

The following details how you can conduct market research over the Internet.

Pick your industry. Let's say you wanted to open a florist shop. Begin by typing "florist" into the best search engine there is, Google <www.google.com>. Doing this will yield many hyperlinks from which to choose. You can begin by exploring various links that look good. For example, the Ohio Florists Association link might look interesting. At this Web site, you will find an area of industry links that will open up the world of flowers to you—associations, government, colleges and universities, floriculture magazines. Everything you need to know about the florist business is but a few clicks away.

Make it more specific. You will likely need information more specific and germane to your geographic area. You can find this on the Net too. Here are several sites that can give you industry-specific market research:

- <www.inside.com> The home of *American Demographics,* a monthly magazine that offers accurate information on emerging consumer trends, analysis of those trends, and issues and events that relate to consumer markets. The site and the magazine contain detailed insights into spending, growth, and demographics. You have to pay a minimal fee for the content.
- <www.hoovers.com> Hoover's offers company, industry, and market intelligence, as well as sales, marketing, business development, and other intelligence on public and private companies worldwide. It is a great business information resource. This is also a fee-for-content site.
- <www.marketresearch.com> This great site offers a search of the largest database of market research publications. Over 50,000 titles from more than 350 leading publishers. The site is organized into 21 different industry categories, and offers a slew of market research information.
- <www.marketresearch.org.uk> The Market Research Society is one of the largest international organizations for those interested in market, social, and opinion research. This site can help you head in the right direction.
- <www.marketingpower.com> This is the site of the American Marketing Association. A great site for an overview of marketing in general, and for specific market research.

Combined, all of these sources should enable you to decide if there is really a market for the business you want to create. When you have firmly concluded that you have a good idea and are convinced that there is a market for your business, the next step is to draft a business plan that will explain exactly how you plan to tap this market and make money.

The Business Plan

I bet you don't want to draft a business plan. Maybe you are thinking that you know what you are going to do and consider it as a waste of time. Possibly you have your funding in place so you figure that no one is ever going to read it, so why bother. I don't blame you. Business plans are a lot of work and you may, in fact, be the only person who ever reads it. But it is still an important exercise nonetheless.

Think of it this way: An experienced pilot would not fly anywhere without a detailed, well-researched flight plan. The plan helps him understand where he is going and how he will get there. Just as you wouldn't trust a new pilot to fly you and your family to an unknown destination without some assurances that he planned the trip, knew where he was going, and knew how to get there, you shouldn't trust that you can start a business without a plan.

A business plan is your flight plan, your game plan. It is your blueprint. Creating one forces you to carefully think through the entire enterprise—from products, prices, and income projections to advertising, marketing, and sales forecasts. By analyzing some things that you are probably unfamiliar and uncomfortable with, you are forced to really understand what you are getting into and how much money you can realistically expect to make. If you don't create a plan, your entire enterprise will be a shot in the dark and you are going to be investing too much of your time, money, reputation, and ego to wander around in the dark, hoping your business will work. That is why you need a plan.

Business Plan Overview

A business plan is a written summary of what you hope to accomplish by being in business and how you intend to organize your resources to meet your goals. In it, you define your basic product, your income objectives, your management team, your competition, and your specific operating procedures. It details the what, when, where, why, and how of your business. It explains what your objectives are, why your business will be unique, and the steps you will take to achieve those objectives. In essence, it is the road map for operating your business and measuring progress along the way.

There are many practical advantages of a business plan:

- It identifies the amount of financing or outside investment required, when it is needed, and how it will be used.
- It enables a lender or investor to assess your financing proposal and assess you as a business manager.
- By committing your plans to paper, your overall ability to manage the business will improve. You will know your business better. You will be able to look ahead and hopefully avoid problems before they arise.
- A business plan forces you to be realistic and avoid pie-in-the-sky projections.
- It helps you to identify your customers, your market, your pricing strategy, and your competition.

> You don't want your business plan to be so short that it doesn't include the necessary information or so long that you have to spend a lot of time rewriting it. A normal business plan should be between 30 and 50 pages. Not more, not less.

Elements of a Business Plan

While every business plan is different because every business is different, they are all generally alike. Your business plan should include the following elements.

Executive Summary

The document starts with an executive summary describing the highlights of the business plan. Even though your entire business is well described later on, a crisp, three- or four-page introduction helps to capture the immediate attention of the potential investor or lender. The executive summary is just that—a compact summary of the whole plan. In it, you should explain

- what sort of company it is,
- what your product or service will be,
- why your business will be unique,
- whom the management team is comprised of, and
- how much money you need, in what stages, and how you will use it.

It is important that this summary be your best. Remember, this may be the only chance you have to attract attention. Some people say that busy lenders read only the executive summary; if it doesn't grab them by the lapels, they move on to the next plan. Make sure your executive summary sells your idea so the reader will retain interest and continue reading. Because the executive summary is so important, you might want to write it last, after you have thought through the entire plan.

Table of Contents

Right after the executive summary will be a table of contents that lists the section titles and page numbers for easy reference.

Description of Business Venture

This is the heart of your plan. In it, you will describe exactly what your business is going to be and how you envision it proceeding. This section will contain:

- A description of your product or service. What is it? How is it different? Why will people want it? Why isn't someone else doing it? What kind of equipment will you need? Do you have or can you get a patent? The thing you must do is put yourself in a potential investor's place and ask yourself what he or she would need to know before investing in your business.
- A description of your business. Is this a wholesale business, retail, professional, or what?

Market Analysis

This is where all of that research comes in handy. Here you will identify your target market—your typical customers. You will also explain present buying patterns and offer trends, projected growth, customer behavior, complementary products or services, barriers to entry into the marketplace, and so on. Tell the reader what the total market is for your industry. For example: The computer repair market in the United States grew to more than $1 billion last year.

Next define your target market. If your business is going to be confined to your specific locale, then you need to explain what the market is like in your area. After this, you must narrow your market down even more and analyze what your total feasible market is. Finally, you must determine what your share of that feasible market will be. This is called your market share.

How will you capture that market share? That is what you need to know and what you need to convey. How will you position your goods or services in the market? What will your pricing strategy be? How will you promote yourself and your business? You should include in this section your sales strategy (sales objectives, target customers, sales tools, and sales support), distribution plan (direct to public, wholesale, or retail), pricing structure (mark-ups, margins, and break-even), and promotion plan (media, advertising, promotions, and publicity).

Description of the Industry

This section will include statistics and information about your chosen industry. You want to include the following in this section:

- Industry outlook and growth potential, such as industry trends, new products and developments, etc.
- Markets and customers, including the size of the total market and market trends
- National and economic trends, such as population shifts, consumer trends, and relevant economic indicators

Researching and writing this section will enable you to understand the industry you are getting involved in much better.

Business Goals

Explain in this section where you see your company in one year, in two years, and so on up until the fifth year. Explain specifically how you will reach these goals and what will happen in different economic environments.

> Do you want your business to get funded? Then write your business plan in plain English. Nothing turns off a reader more than lots of technical jargon that he or she cannot understand.

Competition

This section of your business plan should include all pertinent information about your competition, including the length of time they have been in business, where they are located, and what their average annual sales are. You will want to analyze the following:

- The reasons behind their success
- What they do right and wrong
- What customers are looking for
- How those needs are being met by your competitors
- How those needs are not being met

The Internet sites listed in the Secondary Research section can help you fill in this information. Getting some good, solid data about your competitors will impress investors and teach you plenty in the process.

In addition, you should explain how you perceive your business will compete in terms of strengths and weaknesses compared to the strengths and weaknesses of these competitors. Explain how you intend to overcome your competition and your expectations of the impact your company will have on their business. Consider how well your competition satisfies the needs of potential customers. Determine how you fit into this picture and what niche you plan to fill. Will you offer a better location, convenience, a better price, later hours, better quality, or better service?

Management Team

What are your qualifications and those of your team? Do not underestimate the importance an investor puts in the management team. Banks, angels, and venture capital firms will want to see that you have a board of directors or officers with a record of entrepreneurial success—proven business leaders, people with legal and finance skills, marketing experts, and the like. Those types of people will help prove the viability of your business and can make all the difference between funding and no funding. The resumes of all key personnel should be included in this section as well.

Sales Forecast

The next part of the business plan covers sales, operations, and finances. This section deals with hard numbers and forecasts of sales, operating expenses, profits, and the like. This section should include:

- A monthly forecast for coming year (sales volume in units and dollars)
- An annual forecast for the following two to four years (sales volume in dollars)
- Assumptions on which you base these forecasts

By this point, your research on the competition is vital. Analyze their location, customer volumes, traffic patterns, hours of operation, busy periods, prices, quality of their goods and services, product lines carried, promotional techniques, positioning, and product catalogues and other handouts. If feasible, talk to customers and sales staff.

Use this research to estimate your sales on a monthly basis for your first year. The basis for your sales forecast can be the average monthly sales of a similar-sized competitor's business that is operating in a similar market.

Financial Analysis

A business plan is not just words; it is words *and* numbers. You need to understand and explain how much it will cost to get your business up and running, and how much it will cost to keep it going on a monthly basis. The financial needs of the plan depend greatly on your marketing and sales strategies. They all must fit together. Remember, though, that while projections are projections, they must show an understanding of how all of the variables of the business plan fit together. In the end, you must really understand the numbers because investors will grill you on them.

In this section, you are also going to explain how much money you are asking for and how you will be spending it. This section will include a spreadsheet that analyzes income and expenses for the next few years, including:

- *Profit and loss statement (P&L).* This is a summary of your projected business transactions over a period of time. It explains the difference between your income and expenses. An income statement is the same as the profit and loss statement. Your P&L will include analyses of sales by month, gross profit and profit margin, overhead, depreciation, interest payable on any loans, and net profit.
- *Cash flow statement.* This statement shows how much cash your business will need, when it will be needed, and where it will come from. Do you need to buy inventory? How much will that cost every month? What are your receipts, bills, wages paid, etc.? That is what you will be discussing here. The cash flow statement is important because it forces you to realistically look at the bottom line and see if you are making (or are going to make) enough money to service your debts. A cash flow statement is a great tool that you should use throughout your business career as it is a mirror of where things are.

- *Balance sheet.* The balance sheet forecasts your assets and liabilities. It shows your financial position at a fixed point in time, usually at the end of the year. It helps you understand where all the money coming into the business has come from and where it has gone. Balance sheet information is extracted mostly from the P&L and cash flow statement.

This section is often the most difficult part of a business plan for many entrepreneurs. It's easy to wax poetic about your fantastic business idea and how it will make everyone rich. Actually putting hard numbers to those projections is not always easy, but you have to do it. You have to crunch some realistic numbers to go along with your realistic (and hopefully enthusiastic) plan.

Where do you get this information? There are many sources of information to assist you. Some key sources are competitors, trade suppliers, business associations, trade associations, trade publications, and trade directories. Once you have this information, you will need to provide it in your financial statement.

■ Ray's Computer Repair

Projected Profit & Loss Statement

Projected Income (1/1/03—12/31/03)	$74,590
Projected Expenses	
Auto	$ 1,500
Bank fees	250
Conference	490
Equipment	1,020
Insurance	2,800
Marketing	6,200
Phone	1,900
Postage	400
Printing	900
Supplies	14,900
Taxes	6,800
Projected Total Expenses	37,160
Projected Net Profit	$37,430

The financial section of your business plan will also analyze the use of any loan proceeds you are seeking, including the amount of the loan, the term, and when it is required. Finally, you need to disclose your financial situation and how much you will personally be contributing to the venture. The appendix of your plan should include the past three years' income tax returns. Also include a current credit report.

Critical Risks

This section will analyze what you consider to be the biggest risks and obstacles to the success of the business and how you plan to overcome them.

Action Plan

This section will contain specific steps you will take to accomplish this year's goals and checkpoints for measuring results. Identify significant dates, sales levels, and production levels as decision points.

Appendix

This section will contain:

- Substantiation documentation, articles of interest, etc.
- References
- Name of present lending institution
- Names of your lawyer and accountant
- Personal net worth statement
- Tax returns
- Resumes
- Letters of intent (potential orders, customer commitments, letters of support)

Mistakes to Avoid

Preparing a business plan will generate a lot of thought and a lot of paper. You will need to write it and rewrite it. But the process should do you a lot of good. In the end, you will have a much better idea about how your business will run, what it will take to succeed, and what risks will be involved in the process.

As you write it, try to avoid making common mistakes, such as off-the-mark projections for net profit and other economic numbers. You cannot simply pull numbers out of thin air. You have to do your homework and locate numbers that realistically project your expenses and profits. Another common mistake is using income projections that are inconsistent with the industry norm or that don't generate enough cash flow to service the debt.

THE BOTTOM LINE

In the end, all this work will all be worth it. Either you will be able to get a loan because you clearly know what you are doing as demonstrated in the plan, or you will have learned a great deal about how to make your business fly. Either way, you are a winner.

Resources You Can Use

BusinessPlans.org
2013 Wells Branch Parkway, #305
Austin, TX 78728
<www.businessplans.org>

Small Business Development Centers (SBDC)
<www.sba.gov/gopher/Local-Information/Small-Business-Development-Centers/>

<www.bizplanit.com>

<www.paloalto.com>

6

Choosing Great Names and Locations

Now that you have a good idea about what your business is going to be and where you are headed with it, it is time to begin to put your foundation in place. You will need to structure the business legally, get the necessary licenses and permits, and get funding. But before you can do any of those things, it is time to have some fun. You need to name your business and, in all likelihood, find a location for it.

What's in a Name?

Naming your business should be enjoyable, but for some people, it is stressful. What if you pick the wrong name? What if the name you pick has already been taken? While it is smart to be cautious, it is nothing to get overly concerned about. The important thing to realize is that your business name will become your alter ego, so be sure to pick a name that reflects on you and your business well.

How do you pick a name? You have three options. The first is to pick a name that says exactly what your business is. Begin with what your business is going to do and the image you want to express. Include both in the actual name of the business or reflect those ideas in the name, so that when people hear your business name, they know what you are offering. Using this method, you want a name that says what you do and is easy to remember, for example, Mr. Plumber, Borders Bookstore and Café, or CompUSA. By the same token, you might want the business name to express the benefits that people will get by patronizing the business, such as Jiffy Lube or Quickee Mart. Here's a great one that utilizes both image and benefits—Baja Fresh.

Be sure the name is not already in local use and that it is not too similar to that of a competitor. Try to pick one that is catchy and memorable; alliteration often works well. Also, be sure to pick a name that is not difficult to pronounce or spell. When people call directory assistance, you want them to be able to find you. When Nolan Bushnell invented the first popular video game—Pong—he wanted to name his company Syzygy. Luckily for him, that name was already taken, so he settled on Atari instead (a word used in the Japanese game GO to warn opponents that they are about to be conquered).

✎ Picking a Name

What sort of business is it? _____

What will be the distinguishing characteristics of the business? _____

What benefits will people get by coming to the business? _____

List five adjectives that will describe the business: _____

How will it be different than similar businesses? _____

What are the names of similar businesses? _____

What are the good and bad things about those names? _____

Based on the above, come up with five possible names for your business:

1. _____

2. _____

3. _____

4. _____

5. _____

■ **Real Life Example**

Walt Disney's first business was an animation studio called Laugh-O-Grams, a company that would go bankrupt after only one year, in 1923. After the bankruptcy of Laugh-O-Grams, Walt moved to California to be closer to his brother Roy, who was recuperating from tuberculosis. Undeterred by Walt's recent failure, Roy and Walt formed Disney Brothers Studios and set up their first animation studio in their garage. Although they quickly got a contract to create an animated character called Oswald the Lucky Rabbit, this business too was soon in trouble after Walt unknowingly sold the rights to Oswald to the distributor. Walt Disney was on the verge of bankruptcy again.

Desperate, on a train trip from New York back to Los Angeles, Walt decided to create a new character, one he would own, one with a more memorable name than Oswald, a character he hoped would save his troubled studio. That character was, of course, Mickey Mouse.

After you come up with five names that you really like, get some feedback from people you trust; they may not think your name is as good as you think it is. Remember, your business has to serve a market need, so finding out what the market thinks about your proposed business name, even in a small and informal way, is smart.

The second method of business-name creation is to pick a name that is totally unique and has nothing to do with your business at all, such as Amazon .com or Xerox. These names are great because they are so unique that they are memorable. The risk here is that while your name may be unique, it may be too odd and obscure for people to remember it. One reason Amazon.com and Xerox are memorable names is because those companies had the wherewithal to get people to remember them and, in the process, brand their name. If you do not have a sizable marketing budget, picking an obscure name can be more of a curse than a blessing.

The last method for creating a winning business name is to hire someone to name it for you. There are companies whose business is to come up with company and product names, and they are often fond of coining new words for names. They usually do a great job of coming up with a unique, memorable name, and get paid handsomely for their efforts—$50,000 is not

> *Branding* is not the same thing as a business name. A brand incorporates much more than that. In essence, a brand is a company's image, logo, products, and name all rolled into one. What do you think of when you think of Nike? Probably athletic shoes, the swoosh, athletes, exercise, and "Just do it." Your brand is what customers think of when they think of your business. Branding is a process that builds awareness of your name via advertising and marketing.

uncommon. For the right business, it may be a smart marketing move and a worthwhile investment. For others, the cost is not worth whatever results you get. It's a balancing act between budgetary restraints and need.

Trademark Concerns

While making your final decision regarding your name, it is important to do a trademark search to see if the name already has been trademarked. If it has, you may not be able to use it. Different names are given different degrees of trademark protection. A trademark is a distinctive word, phrase, or logo that is used to identify a business. Nike and its unique swoosh symbol are protected under trademark law because they are distinctive.

Other words are given far less protection. Common or ordinary words that are not inherently distinctive get much less, or no, trademark protection, even if someone tries to trademark them. Examples of such common, nondistinctive business names include:

- Sam's Auto
- Western Dairy
- Quick Computers

If you think there is a chance someone may usurp your company name, catch phrase, symbol, or design, then you need a trademark. Trademarks are used to identify and protect your product or brand.

Don't make the mistake of thinking you don't need trademark protection. Any growing business usually does. Consider the case of Spencer, who opened a furniture store in 1960. His sons joined him in the business in the early 1980s. By 1990, their enterprise, Spencer's Furniture Galleria, had grown to 14 stores in three states. In 1997, Spencer and his sons tried to register a trademark on the name only to find that the name Spencer's Furniture Galleria had been trademarked nine years earlier by someone else. When asked what that meant, Spencer's lawyer explained that Spencer actually had no right to use the name Spencer's Furniture Galleria because it constituted trademark infringement.

The name was valuable enough to Spencer and his sons that they asked their lawyer to straighten out the mess. After doing some research, the lawyer found out that the owner of the trademark never used the mark and was willing to sell it for $5,000. It was an expensive lesson.

Federal registration provides a number of significant benefits, including:

- Nationwide notice of trademark ownership
- Evidence of and a presumption of ownership of the name or symbol

So yes, you do want to register your name and logo. The good news is that doing so shouldn't be difficult or expensive. It is now easier than ever to register a trademark without an attorney—the whole process can be done online. Most of the information you need can be obtained at the U.S. Patent and Trademark Office (USPTO) Web site, <www.uspto.gov>. The USPTO site answers your basic questions and enables you to do an online trademark search. You also can access forms and submit the application online.

In the end, the lesson for any entrepreneur naming a business is to be smart, pick well, and do your homework.

Location

As mentioned in Chapter 3, not all businesses need a great location. Retail businesses need to be in an area where there is a lot of walk-by or drive-by traffic, but not all businesses have such requirements. The Old Spaghetti Factory always seems to have its locations near a railroad, and you can bet one reason is because they pay much less for those properties. So there are many things to consider.

When selecting a location, you must first determine how important foot and car traffic will be to your business. A high-profile location is important when impulse buying is part of your plan. Thus, a gas station needs a great location with a lot of traffic; a dentist does not.

✏ Retail Business Checklist

The things you want to consider when looking at a location are:

- [ ] **Population and demographics.** Will there be enough people to support the business? What has been the reaction and fate of similar businesses in the area?

- [ ] **Traffic.** You want the site to be near some centers of activity. My father owned a chain of carpet stores when I was growing up, and he loved to be across the street from malls. He figured that he got the benefit of the mall's advertising and traffic, but without the high rent of actually being in the mall. Is there public transportation nearby?

- [ ] **Competition.** Where is your competition located? Fast-food restaurants often like being bunched together, but a print shop usually likes to be the only one in the neighborhood. Are there too many competitors nearby?

- [ ] **Visibility.** Make sure your potential location is visible from major roads.

- [ ] **Signs.** You need to be sure that there are no restrictions in the lease or the law that will limit your ability to post adequate signs for your new business.

- [ ] **Zoning.** The spot, obviously, needs to be zoned for your type of business (see explanation later in this chapter).

- [ ] **Appearance.** Is there adequate parking? Is there a bathroom for the public? Make sure the place is landscaped well, has adequate outdoor lighting, and has appropriate businesses nearby.

- [ ] **Interior design.** A well-designed display of merchandise can make shopping easier for the customer and boost sales. Be sure to review the flow of customer traffic. A free-flowing pattern has better visual appeal and allows customers to move around, while aisles offer better merchandise presentation.

- [ ] **History.** Some locations seem to be jinxed. You know the ones. No matter what business moves into that location, it seems to last for six months before closing up shop. Avoid these locations because no matter what you do, the local clientele will already have preconceived notions about your business.

> ☐ **Rent.** Leases will be discussed in detail later in the chapter, but suffice it to say, you want to be sure that you can afford the location you want. This is where your business plan will become invaluable. If you avoided pie-in-the-sky projections, then you know exactly how much rent you can afford. Avoid picking a location simply because the rent is cheap; that should not be your main consideration. While keeping your overhead low is indeed a key to success in business (see Chapter 20), a cheap, bad location is similarly a key to failure.
>
> ☐ **Image.** Your storefront is your window to the world. Make sure yours represents the image you want people to have, the brand you are trying to create.

Indeed, an out-of-the-way location can be a great choice for certain businesses. Opening in a redeveloping urban area, for example, may allow you to benefit from tax breaks or a grateful consumer base. Generally, if you are selling commonplace items (food, groceries, clothes, etc.), location is probably more important to you. If you are selling services or specialized products, location should be less of a concern.

There are many different sorts of locations that may have all of these questions already answered, such as shopping centers. While a shopping center or mall can be a great spot for many businesses, you must weigh the benefits against the high cost of doing business in that location. Make sure you will be able to make a profit.

An entrepreneur who is starting a manufacturing or wholesale business will have different considerations. While such a business may be set up in a more remote location, you want to be sure that you are close enough to town that transportation hubs and services are within fairly easy access. Be sure that the place is zoned for your type of business. Also make sure there is adequate cell phone coverage in the area and that you have access to other necessary services. Other things you might want to consider include:

- Does the building have restroom facilities and break rooms?
- Can employees and suppliers get there easily?
- Is there a shipping and receiving area?
- Are there enough phone jacks and electrical outlets?

- Are there any environmental issues to consider?
- Does the facility comply with the Americans with Disabilities Act?
- Is there room to expand?

Is yours going to be a professional office? You can rent space in a professional office building or go to an executive suite. Executive suites are small office spaces in office buildings that individuals or small companies can rent. Typically, each tenant has an individual office and shares the services of the executive suite's receptionist and use of the suite's joint conference room, copier, postage machine, and other office equipment. All you do is move in and everything you need to conduct business is already in place. Your company is guaranteed a professional image from the start because executive suites are usually located in high-profile office buildings. You also will have a receptionist to answer your company's phone professionally. All in all, it's a pretty good deal.

■ Understanding Square Feet

Most commercial office or retail space is quoted by square foot per year. A 1,000-square-foot retail space with an asking price of $15 per square foot would cost $15,000 per year, or $1,250 per month. This price may or may not include taxes, insurance, utilities, water, and other related expenses, so be sure to find out what the quote includes.

Locations and Legal Considerations

Whatever location you choose, you must never sign the lease or purchase the property without being absolutely certain that it will be legal for you to operate the business you want in that location. There are several different things to consider:

- *Zoning.* Cities usually zone buildings and areas into residential, commercial, industrial, and mixed-use areas. You must be sure that the location you want is zoned appropriately for the business you want to start. Check with your city before signing any contract. Luckily, even if it's not zoned as you want, it is possible to get a *variance* from the city. A variance is as the name suggests, a change in the normal rules. Your lawyer can help with this.

- *Other legal issues.* Find out if there are other legal restrictions that may affect your business. For example, some municipalities limit the number of certain types of business, such as cafes or fast food franchises, to certain areas. Other restrictions may require that your business provide off-street parking, close at a certain time, or limit the size and type of signs you may have. Your city should have a business development office that can answer these sorts of questions.
- *Contract restrictions.* In malls and other retail complexes, the lease or CC&R (covenants, conditions, and restrictions) may limit what you can do. For example, in certain shopping centers, there may be a limit of no more than one news kiosk or two burger joints.
- *Home office restrictions.* If you are starting a home-based business, contact your city to find out what sort of occupational license and other licenses you may need. Zoning regulations may limit the number

---

Location Worksheet

1. For population information on this area, I contacted:

   ☐ Real estate agents   ☐ Local planning and zoning boards

   ☐ Census data   ☐ Chamber of commerce

2. The population is:
   a. Steady
   b. Growing
   c. Declining

3. The residents in the area are (check all that apply):

   ☐ College aged / Young adults   ☐ Middle-aged

   ☐ Young families   ☐ Elderly

   (Continued)

✎ Location Worksheet (Continued)

4. The income levels in this area are:
   a. Lower
   b. Middle
   c. Upper

5. The three major types of businesses in the area are: _____

6. The number of new businesses opened during the past year is: _____

7. "Anchor" tenants and other major draws to the area are: _____

8. Name, address, and proximity of each competitor:

   a. _____

   b. _____

   c. _____

9. For each potential location, answer the following:

   Traffic area: ☐ High   ☐ Low

   Easy access to: ☐ Transportation hubs and freeways ☐ Bus lines ☐ Pedestrians

   Adequate signage? ☐ Yes ☐ No

   Safe from crime and other hazards? ☐ Yes ☐ No

   Condition of the building: ☐ Poor ☐ Fair ☐ Good ☐ Excellent

   Is there sufficient: ☐ Display areas ☐ Fixtures ☐ Infrastructure ☐ Work areas

   ☐ Office space ☐ Storage ☐ Restrooms ☐ Break areas

   ☐ Shipping and receiving ☐ Parking ☐ Room to grow

   Other features that make this location attractive: _____

   The length of the lease is: _____

   The total cost per month (including utilities, security, insurance, etc.) is: _____

of customers you can have, the signs you can erect, or even the type of business you can start.

Negotiating the Lease

Negotiating a lease with a landlord is not all that different than negotiating the purchase of a car. The important thing to know is what price you want going into the deal and remember the rule: *Everything is negotiable*. The lease you are given is simply a starting point.

If you are at the stage where you are negotiating over lease terms, then you have become a valuable commodity to the landlord. Finding qualified businesses that are willing and able to take on a commercial lease payment is not simple. Accordingly, you may be in the power position when negotiating a lease and you can ask the landlord for concessions and changes to the lease, as necessary.

You do so by doing your homework first. Find out how much the rent is in similar spaces. Is the vacancy rate high or low in this area? If it's high, you can negotiate a great deal because the landlord needs you. If the space is vacant, find out how long it has been vacant (the longer the better for you). The more you know, the better equipped you will be to negotiate a good deal.

Once you are presented with the lease, read it carefully and then give it to your lawyers for review. If you find some part of the lease that you or your lawyers don't like, negotiate that point. Remember that the lease was drawn up by your potential landlord's lawyer and will certainly favor your landlord. Remember too that although you might be presented with a preprinted lease that may seem difficult to change, it is nothing more than a contract, and the essence of contract law is that both sides must agree to all conditions. That, in fact, is why a contract is also called an agreement. If you don't agree, it can be changed.

Above all, try to cultivate a good working relationship with your landlord. That will go further toward working out problems than a dozen letters from your lawyer.

✎ Lease Negotiating Checklist

Make sure you understand and agree to the following:

☐ **The length of the lease.** You want it long enough to establish your business, but not so long that you are locked in if your venture doesn't work out. A year or two with an option for a renewal is a good idea.

☐ **The lease payments.** Getting one or more months free is not unheard of when signing a long-term lease.

☐ **Gross or net lease.** Determine whether the lease will be gross or net. A gross lease is one where the landlord pays for taxes, insurance, janitors, and utilities.

☐ **Cap increases.** Be sure that your lease limits the amount your landlord can increase your rent. Five percent a year is typical. What are the terms of the renewal?

☐ **Bail-out clause.** Especially in a retail lease, make sure that the agreement allows you to get out of it if your sales do not reach a predetermined level. Similarly, a *cotenancy clause* allows you out of the contract if an anchor tenant nearby leaves.

☐ **Other obligations.** Make sure you understand all of your obligations under the lease.

Do not sign any commercial lease without having an attorney review it, period.

Resources You Can Use

International Institute of Site Planning
202-546-2322
715 G Street, SE
Washington, DC 20002
<www.arcat.com/index.cfm>

THE BOTTOM LINE

Both choosing a name and picking a location are double-edged swords. Sure it's fun, but a mistake in either area can doom your business. Your name should reflect your business and be memorable. Your location must be chosen with care, be affordable, be zoned properly, and be accessible to your customers.

SBA Business Names and Licenses
<www.sba.gov/hotlist/businessnames.html>

The United States Patent and Trademark Office
Crystal Plaza 3, Room 2C02
Washington, DC 20231

C H A P T E R

7

Licenses, Permits, and Business Formation

Deciding what legal form your business should take is not the most scintillating of topics, but it may be one of the most important decisions you will make. The form your business takes can determine how big it may grow, who can invest in it, and who is responsible should it get in trouble. It is a critical decision. Once decided, it is then important to handle some other legal issues, namely getting the requisite licenses and permits required by your city, county, or state.

Business Formation

There are three forms your business can take. It can be a sole proprietorship, a partnership, or a corporation, and each of the last two have subsets. When deciding which of these is best for you, it would behoove you to speak with both your lawyer and your account, because each choice has different legal and financial considerations to weigh. Below is an overview that you can use as a launching pad for discussions with your own advisors.

Sole Proprietorships and General Partnerships

A sole proprietorship is the cheapest and easiest form of business you can start. Simply decide on a name for your business, get a business license, file and publish a fictitious business name statement, hang your shingle, and voilà! You are in business. Creating a sole proprietorship shouldn't cost more than $100.

The downside to sole proprietorship is significant: You and the business are legally the same thing. If something goes wrong, say as a chiropractor you accidentally injure someone, not only is your business at risk, but so are your personal assets. Your home, cars, bank accounts, everything is at risk when you are a sole proprietor. Another problem with this form of business is that you have no partners to work with or bounce ideas off of. It is a dangerous way to do business.

Therefore, having a teammate is why operating a business as a partnership is attractive. Essentially, a business partnership is a lot like a marriage. You need to pick a good partner because you will be spending a lot of time together and trusting each other. And, as with a sole proprietorship, in a general partnership, both you and your partner are personally liable for the debts of the business. The danger is that your partner can make some dumb decisions and get the partnership into debt, and you will be personally responsible for that debt.

So, as you can see, while there are many good aspects to having a partner, partnerships are fraught with danger. You have to weigh the benefits against the burdens and decide if bringing in a partner is right for you.

Another thing to be wary of is the emotional aspect of having a partner. One advantage to being a sole proprietor, and thus the only boss, is you have no one to answer to except yourself. That's one of the definite perks of being a solo entrepreneur. Bringing in a partner means you will have to consider another point of view before any major decision is made. Also, when partnerships do not work out, best friends who become partners do not always stay best friends.

On the other side of the ledger, there are many things to be said for having a business partner. One is that it enables you to have someone with whom to brainstorm. That great idea you have may not be such a great idea after all, and a partner you trust can tell you why. A partner also gives you another pair of hands to do the work. It is difficult to be the one who has to do everything when you are solo. Partners alleviate that. Last, and certainly not least, having a business partner gives you someone to share the financial responsibilities of the business. That is not insignificant.

Having considered the pros and cons, having concluded that a partner can help more than it might hurt, and maybe even knowing someone you would like to partner with, it is still a good idea that you "date" first before jumping in. Find a project or two and work together. See how you get along, how your styles mesh (or don't), how you deal with deadlines, and whether the union enhances your work. Remember, you will be spending a lot of time with your partner, so you need to be sure that you work well together, have a good time, and have skills that complement one another.

Finally, get some work references and make some phone calls. Deciding to partner with someone is one of the most important decisions you can make in your small business, so don't skimp on the homework. As far as the costs go, the licensing and permits are fairly insignificant. The main cost is hiring a business lawyer to draft the partnership agreement. That can run anywhere from $1,000 to $2,500.

Limited Partnerships

There are two classes of partnerships: general partnerships (discussed above) and limited partnerships. In a general partnership, all partners are equal. Each partner has equal power to incur obligations on behalf of the partnership, and each partner has unlimited liability for the debts of that partnership. Because not all partnerships require that the partners have equal power and liabilities, some partnerships decide to form as a limited partnership instead.

In a limited partnership, there is usually only one general partner (although there could be more). The other partners are called limited partners, hence the name limited partnership. In a limited partnership, the general partner or partners have full management responsibility and control of the partnership business on a day-to-day basis. The general partner runs the show and makes the decisions. A limited partner cannot incur obligations on behalf of the partnership and does not participate in the daily operations and management of the partnership. In fact, the participation of a limited partner in the partnership is usually nothing more than initially contributing capital and hopefully later receiving a proportionate share of the profits. A limited partner is essentially a passive investor.

While the general partner has all of the power, he or she also has the lion's share of the liability. A limited partner's liability is capped at the amount of his or her financial contribution to the partnership. Should the truck of a limited partnership kill someone accidentally, the damaged party could go after the general partner's personal assets, but would be limited to the limited partner's capital contribution.

Thus, the main advantage to this business entity is that it allows the general partner the freedom to run the business without interference, and gives the limited partners diminished liability if things go wrong. Although a limited partner may seek to be more involved in the day-to-day operations of the partnership, he or she does so at some risk. If he or she does participate more, it is altogether possible that he or she may be viewed as a general partner in the eyes of the law, with its attendant liability risks.

Another key benefit of the limited partnership is that it pays no income tax. Income and losses are attributed proportionally to each partner and accounted for on their respective tax returns. Because of this flow-through tax treatment, a limited partnership is often the structure of choice for real estate ventures and investment securities groups.

If you do decide to start your business as a limited partnership, have your partnership agreement drafted by an attorney. Again, the costs will likely run between $1,000 and $2,500. You might also want to read *Let's Go Into Business Together: 8 Secrets to Successful Business Partnering* by Azriela Jaffe.

Incorporating

The best thing about forming your business as a corporation is that it limits your personal liability, which is not true for partnerships and sole proprietorships. For example, say that you owned a tire shop and one of your employees negligently installed a tire that fell off a car and caused a three-car accident with several personal injuries. If your tire store was not a corporation, the injured parties could come after you personally for monetary damages. This means that you could lose your business, your house—everything. That would not be true if you incorporated. Creditors are limited to the assets of the corporation only for payment and may not collect directly from the shareholders.

There are several types of corporations including limited liability companies, closely held corporations, professional corporations, and S and C corporations.

■ Pros and Cons of Incorporating

Pros

- The corporation limits one's personal liability.

- The corporation is a separate legal entity. It has its own tax identification number and is its own legal entity, separate and apart from the owners.

- Sole proprietorships and partnerships normally end upon death, disability, bankruptcy, or retirement of the proprietor or a partner. Corporations, being a separate legal entity, do not cease to exist when one of the founding members leaves.

- As the corporation grows, management and ownership can be separated so that the business can continue and the owners can still reap benefits. However, they may choose not to run the corporation.

- An important corporate characteristic is the ability to consolidate, merge, or buy other corporations.

- You may be taken more seriously by others if you have a corporation.

- Corporate stock may be freely transferred by sale or gift.

- A corporation can buy and sell property in the corporate name.

- A corporation can contract with the government, whereas most other business entities cannot.

- A corporation has numerous tax advantages, including pension and profit-sharing options, and the election of S corporation status (see the following section).

Cons

- It is expensive to create and, depending on the situation, to maintain. Incorporating may cost $1,000 to $10,000, depending on the type and complexity.

- Majority shareholders can overpower minority shareholders.

- The shareholders, as owners, have little say in day-to-day operations.

- A corporation is subject to greater governmental regulation and control than other types of business entities.

Limited Liability Companies

Limited liability companies (or LLCs) combine many of the advantages of a corporation and a partnership without the disadvantages. The LLC is a fairly recent business entity that may offer greater business and tax advantages than a regular corporation, while also offering better business and structuring advantages than a partnership.

Like a corporation, an LLC provides the limited personal liability that is so attractive in corporations, along with being a separate legal entity that can sue and be sued as well as buy and own property. Similar to a corporation, articles of incorporation must be filed with the state, and a registered agent must be named for service of process. Like a partnership, shares in the LLC cannot be transferred without the approval of all other members of the LLC.

The death, retirement, expulsion, or bankruptcy of one member does not end the LLC. If all of the remaining members agree, the LLC can continue and, in a few states, the law allows the business to continue with the consent of fewer than all the remaining members.

Closely Held Corporations

Allowed in some states, a close corporation is one whose shares are owned by only a few shareholders. Although there is no specific number, Delaware corporate law states that a close corporation cannot have more than 30 shareholders. Less than 15 is more typical. The purpose of a close corporation is to keep ownership and control within a small group of shareholders who have the same goals.

In a close corporation, distinctions between directors, officers, and shareholders are normally absent as the few owners own and operate the corporation without formalities. Unlike publicly held corporations, a closely held corporation's shares are not traded on the open market.

The advantages to doing business this way are that

- shareholders can be restricted, and
- all shareholders can participate in the business.

The downside is that a few shareholders who disagree with the majority are generally out of luck as they cannot freely sell their shares.

Professional Corporations

This is a certain type of corporation that is designed for professionally licensed entrepreneurs only, and that professional can be the only shareholder. The type of professional that can take part in this plan varies by state, but usually includes doctors, lawyers, dentists, psychologists, and accountants. Note though that a corporation cannot normally shield you from a malpractice award.

S and C Corporations

S corporations are intended for smaller enterprises. Like an LLC, S corporations are informal enough to allow you to run your business like a sole proprietorship or partnership, while giving you the protection of the corporate shield; that is, limited personal liability.

A big disadvantage of regular corporations (or C corporations as they are legally known) is that they are taxed twice—once when profits are realized, and a second time when those profits are passed on to the shareholders. The advantage of the S corporation is that it avoids this double taxation and profits are only taxed once. In fact, S corporations do not pay a corporate tax at all. Instead, their shareholders report profits and losses on their personal tax returns. The advantages of S corporations are obvious, but be aware that there are restrictions:

- An S corporation can have no more than 75 shareholders.
- All shareholders must be citizens or residents of the United States.
- The corporation's tax year must end on December 31.
- It can only have common stock outstanding (as opposed to preferred stock).
- The corporation cannot earn more than 25 percent of its gross income from passive investments such as interest, dividends, royalties, and rents.

To create an S corporation, you must first file the necessary articles of incorporation with your secretary of state's office. You then need to file a Form 2553 with the IRS. This is a fairly complicated matter so it is best to hire qualified legal counsel.

A C corporation is your basic, standard variety, large corporation. GM and Exxon are C corporations. The distinguishing characteristic, and the reason you might want to pick this entity, is that its shares are easily transferable.

Which is best for you? If you plan on creating a large company (one that is publicly traded), you should choose a C corporation because shares of stock are most easily bought or sold. While you might want an S corporation for tax reasons, it is limited to no more than 75 shareholders, all of whom must be individuals, and that is sometimes a problem. LLC's trump S corporations because they have no limit on the number of shareholders, and those shareholders can be corporations and partnerships. Generally speaking, LLC's are best for smaller start-ups and C corporations are best for larger ones.

■ Comparing Business Entities

	Limited Liability	Perpetual Existence	Easy Transferability of Ownership	Separate Legal Entity	Cost
Sole Proprietorship	No	No	No	No	Low
General Partnership	No	No	No	No	Low
Limited Partnership	(Limited partners only)	No	No	No	Medium
LLC	Yes	Yes	Yes	Yes	High
Close Corporation	Yes	Yes	No	Yes	High
S Corporation	Yes	Yes	Yes	Yes	High
Professional Corporation	Yes	No	No	Yes	High
C Corporation	Yes	Yes	Yes	Yes	High

Licenses and Permits

There are some bureaucratic hoops still to jump through before you open your business. If you are going to operate a sole proprietorship or partnership using a name different from your personal name, you are probably required by your city, county, or state to register your fictitious business name, also known as a dba (doing business as). Registering your dba with the proper authorities puts the public on notice that you are the owner of the business. Corporations are not normally required to file a fictitious business name statement, unless they too are operating under a different name. Also, know that some banks require such a statement before opening a business bank account.

Requirements for filing the fictitious business name statement vary according to locale. Some places require that you file a form and pay a fee to the county, others require that you do so with the city. The process usually just requires that you go to the proper office, fill out a fictitious business name statement, and pay a registration fee (usually less than $100). Some places also require that the statement be published in a local newspaper.

You will also need to get a business license from your city or county. Other permits and requirements you may need include:

- A health department permit, if you will be selling food somehow
- Beer, wine, and hard liquor licenses
- Environmental regulations, if you will be using paints or other chemicals, or if you will be burning anything (in a kiln for instance)
- A fire department permit, if your business is going to use flammable materials
- A water pollution control permit, if you will be discharging materials into waterways or sewers
- A permit or permission of a landlord, if you plan on posting a sign of some sort
- A license or bond for certain professions including barbers, lawyers, doctors, nurses, cosmetologists, real estate brokers and agents, mechanics, plumbers, electricians, contractors, and insurance agents

You can begin your journey down the permit path by visiting your city's business planning office. It should have a packet that explains exactly what licenses and permits you need, where to get them, and what they cost.

Resources You Can Use

Findlaw for Business

THE BOTTOM LINE

Dealing with the legalities of your business is not much fun, but you can't overlook it. Working with your lawyer and accountant will help you make the right decisions. In most cases, forming some sort of corporation is in your best interests.

MrAllBiz.com
<www.mrallbiz.com>

Nolo.com
Legal books and software
Phone: 800-728-3555
Fax: 800-645-0895
950 Parker Street
Berkeley, CA 94710-2524
<www.nolo.com>

SBA
Legal and regulatory information

CHAPTER

8

Outfitting the Office

The actual process of setting up your business will involve dealing with plenty of details—details that must be understood and organized before you open the doors; details that must be handled and forgotten so that you can go onto other, more important matters; details that can sink or swim your business.

Aside from creating a winning image (as discussed in Chapter 6), you also need to set up efficient office operations, computer systems, and phone and mail systems. Nailing these details down now will enable you to concentrate on growing your business—a far better use of your time than getting lost in myriad minutiae down the road.

Automating Your Office

Whatever your business, you must computerize it. Whether it involves tracking sales, writing letters, or inventory control, starting out with a good computer system is vital. Although it may seem less expensive to do certain office tasks by hand rather than investing in a good computer system or related software, that is fuzzy logic for two reasons. First, you eventually will automate whatever tasks you begin by hand. Changing over later will take longer and cost more. Second, computer hardware and software will allow you to be more effective and, thus, more productive from the get-go.

Computers represent a solid investment of your start-up capital. Don't skimp in this area. Throughout this book you have been, and will be, cautioned to keep your overhead low. High overhead will eat up your profits and your precious cash flow quickly. But this is not one of those times. The rapid pace of technological change means that computers usually become obsolete within three or four years. If you buy a used one, or an older or a slower model, you are simply speeding up the moment when you will have to buy a new one. Be smart and buy a good computer and the necessary software now.

You have likely learned a thing or two about purchasing computers since you bought your first one. You are more knowledgeable about your computer needs, and you probably know what areas you would like to improve. It may be that your monitor is too small and you want a larger one, or that you want a newer operating system. Probably what you want is speed and more speed.

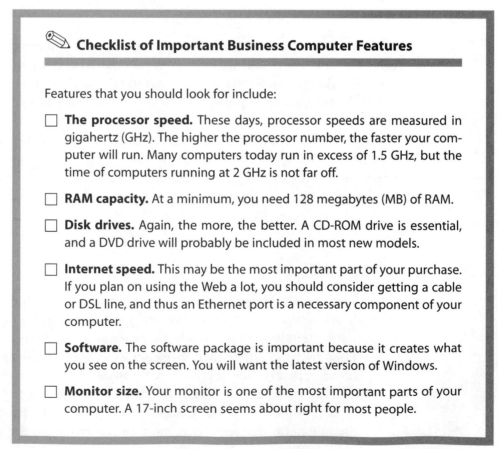

✎ Checklist of Important Business Computer Features

Features that you should look for include:

☐ **The processor speed.** These days, processor speeds are measured in gigahertz (GHz). The higher the processor number, the faster your computer will run. Many computers today run in excess of 1.5 GHz, but the time of computers running at 2 GHz is not far off.

☐ **RAM capacity.** At a minimum, you need 128 megabytes (MB) of RAM.

☐ **Disk drives.** Again, the more, the better. A CD-ROM drive is essential, and a DVD drive will probably be included in most new models.

☐ **Internet speed.** This may be the most important part of your purchase. If you plan on using the Web a lot, you should consider getting a cable or DSL line, and thus an Ethernet port is a necessary component of your computer.

☐ **Software.** The software package is important because it creates what you see on the screen. You will want the latest version of Windows.

☐ **Monitor size.** Your monitor is one of the most important parts of your computer. A 17-inch screen seems about right for most people.

The next question is, where do you buy it? One option is an office super-store. Because of volume buying, superstores can often sell products at 30 per-cent or more below manufacturers' list prices. An even better option is to buy directly from the manufacturer online. Buying from the manufacturer allows you to design the exact system you want. While Gateway <www.gateway .com> and Dell <www.dell.com> began the BTO (built to order) trend, cus-tom computers have caught on with almost every computer maker, and all

■ Leasing Equipment

You can lease not just computers but much of your business equipment. Leasing offers a number of distinct business advantages:

- *Leases are easier to finance than purchases.* Banks will usually want to see two or three years of financial records—records unavailable to a new company—before they will make a loan for equipment. However, leasing companies are not so picky.

- *Leasing improves your cash flow.* It frees up cash. Equipment leases cost less monthly and rarely require down payments (though you may have to pay a security deposit). Conversely, equipment purchase loans usually require down payments of up to 25 percent.

- *Leasing allows you to get more.* Although you might not be able to afford to buy those pricey new tool and dye machines, you might be able to lease them. Even bet-ter: Top-notch equipment can help your people be more productive, create better products, and boost morale.

- *Leasing makes it easier to keep up to date.* If your business relies on new technology, leasing makes a lot of sense. Instead of buying new equipment every two or three years, a series of short-term leases will cost you less and let you upgrade more often.

- *Leasing helps the bottom line.* Some leased assets can be eliminated from your bal-ance sheet, which can improve financial indicators such as your business's debt-to-equity ratio or earnings-to-fixed-assets ratio. Check with your accountant.

If you do decide to lease equipment, keep the term short. A two-year lease is a good idea. You also should try to negotiate a modern equipment substitution clause, which lets you update or exchange your equipment so you do not end up paying for old technology.

the leading PC manufacturers offer their models in just about every configuration imaginable at their online stores.

If your business will require several computer workstations, keep these points in mind:

- Don't fall in love with the technology. If you do, you are liable to make a choice for the wrong reasons. Instead, first decide what your business needs are and *then* look for the computers and other information technology solutions that can fill those needs.
- Once the system is up and running, your people will need to be trained to use it. According to *Inc.,* businesses in the United States spend more than $6 billion on information technology training every year. Seventy-six percent of that training comes from using a traditional instructor, while 17 percent of businesses use videos, satellite TV, or computers. In fact, high-tech training is growing at the rate of 31 percent a year. Interactive training software can also be rented at a cost of between $5,000 and $10,000 for two years. A Web search of "information technology training" will reveal many options.
- You will also need to create a local area network (LAN). By networking all of your computers, you increase productivity and communication within your business. For example, one printer can be shared by five workstations. Everyone can share the same Internet connection. LANs are important.
- You will also need a backup system in case of a calamity, such as a fire or theft. Losing your files could cost you your business.

Software

Many of the routine tasks that entrepreneurs often hate—budgeting, bookkeeping, and billing—can be handled quickly and painlessly with the right software. Software packages exist that can make even the most mundane office tasks tolerable for such jobs as:

- Creating spreadsheets
- Doing payroll
- Invoicing
- Tracking customers
- Tracking sales

- Creating mailers
- Creating form letters
- Calculating taxes

These need not be demanding, time-consuming chores. By automating all of these tasks and scheduling them for a certain time each week or month, you free yourself up to think bigger. Go to your local office supply store and speak with a salesperson about the various suites of software packages available for business owners.

If your business is bigger and requires more than an off-the-shelf solution, the secret is in defining your needs and then educating yourself about your options. Sophisticated (and expensive) IT software is available to solve almost any business problem—inventory control, increasing response rates, securing computer systems, data management, etc. This is what IBM and Microsoft specialize in, as do a host of others. If your needs are along this avenue, contact the company, call your local sales rep, and tell him or her what you need. By being clear up front about what you are looking for, you can avoid buying expensive "solutions" to problems you don't have.

Another option is to hire a software programmer yourself. They can create custom software to suit your exact needs. The downside is that it is usually an expensive proposition and the software often has a few bugs in it that you won't find in commercial software.

Phones and Faxes

It is impossible to generalize about what sort of phone system you may need. A sole proprietor and a corporation will have vastly different needs. As you consider a phone system, ask yourself these questions:

- How much time do I anticipate spending on the phone every day?
- How many people will be using the phone system?
- Will the system need to take messages and forward phone calls?
- Will I need call waiting? Keep in mind many people find it rude.
- Do I want to be able to screen my calls?

If you choose to handle phone duties yourself, you can have a voice mail system or an answering machine pick up you messages when you are not available. The advantage an answering machine has over voice mail is that you can screen your calls when necessary. The advantage of voice mail is that it allows you to have different "mailboxes" if needed, and people are used to using it. Voice mail is offered through your local phone company as well as through private voice mail service bureaus. It is also possible today to set up voice mail on your computer, using specialized software.

If yours is going to be a larger, phone-intensive business, you should definitely consider buying a voice mail system, rather than renting one though your telephone carrier. Personalized voice mail systems can set appointments, take orders, check on deliveries, forward phone calls, and record and retrieve private messages in many mailboxes. Not surprisingly, prices for voice mail systems can run upward of $25,000, although some start as little as $1,000. It is important to make sure that the system you get will neither be obsolete nor inadequate in a year or two.

> One way to get more business is to get a toll-free phone number for your business. Toll free numbers—800, 888, and 877—are not just for the big boys today; almost every sort of business can afford and find uses for a toll-free number. And the easier you make it for people to get a hold of your business, the more business you can generate. There are many options and carriers around today, so prices are competitive. Carriers can be found in your Yellow Pages.

Finally, a fax machine is essential, whatever your business. Fax machines today are not expensive and usually combine a number of very useful functions such as copying and scanning. While Internet faxing services are available, they are not always reliable.

Mail

If you will be running a business that will entail a lot of mail, you should get a postage meter. Available only though rental contracts, postal meters are U.S. Postal Service approved and will mark your envelopes or packages with proper postage. The USPS estimates using a scale along with a postage meter can save businesses up to 20 percent a year in postage costs. And best of all, you can reload your meter over the phone or via the Internet from sites like Stamps.com.

T H E   B O T T O M   L I N E

It will make your life much easier, and your business more successful, if you start out by creating efficient office operations, computer systems, and phone and mail systems. These details are things that can bog you down and waste precious time if not handled properly from the beginning.

Resources You Can Use

Dell
<www.dell.com>

Gateway
<www.gateway.com>

Office Depot
<www.officedepot.com>

Office Max
<www.officemax.com>

Staples
<www.staples.com>

CHAPTER

9

Show Me the Money

Finding the funds to start your business is usually one of the most challenging things the budding entrepreneur will face. Whether yours is a small, home-based business or a large venture that requires six- or seven-figure funding, the good news is that money is available. The bad news is that it is sometimes harder to secure than you may anticipate.

But look around. Every one of those businesses that you see as you drive down the street began as someone's dream and, somehow, those entrepreneurs found the money to open their doors. If they did, so can you.

New businesses normally have a difficult time securing money for a variety of reasons. Conventional financing may be difficult because a new business is a risk to banks—there is no track record or assets to go on. For this reason, almost 75 percent of all start-up businesses are funded through other means. In this chapter, those other options are examined.

Money and the New Business

The very first thing required of you is to accurately estimate the amount of money you need. Taking a cold, hard look at your money requirements will help you know your business better and help ensure your success. Once you know how much capital your business will require, it will be incumbent on you to get it. Having a cash crunch from the start is a sure way to go out of business fast.

Moreover, a realistic budget will help convince a lender or investor that you understand your business and are worth the risk. The first thing any investor will want to know is how much money you will need and how you plan to spend it. They will want specific details on how the money will be spent and how you plan to repay the money.

How Much Money Do You Need?

If you have created a business plan, you should have a pretty good idea how much money you will need to get started. If you haven't figured it out yet, this section will help you. The money you will need can be divided into three categories: one-time costs, working capital, and ongoing costs.

One-time costs are things that you will need to spend money on to start your business but will unlikely see again, such as:

- Legal and accounting costs. You may need to hire a lawyer to help you negotiate contracts, incorporate, or perform other legal services. An accountant may be needed to set up your books.
- Licenses and permits
- Furniture and fixtures
- Decorating and remodeling costs
- Initial inventory
- Security deposits
- Equipment purchases
- Supplies
- Payroll and owner's draw until cash flow is positive

Working capital is the money you will need to keep your business going until you start to make a profit. The old adage "it takes money to make money" is true and real. It is critical to have enough working capital on hand to cover the following costs:

- Debt payments. If you will be borrowing money to get started, you will want to begin repaying it right away.
- Inventory and replacement inventory. Service businesses have little, if any, inventory, but retail and wholesale companies often spend large sums in this area.
- Bills (utilities, suppliers, etc.)
- Advertising and marketing costs (e.g., flyers, sales letters, radio buys, signs, brochures)

- Office supplies, other supplies, cleaning service, etc.
- Ongoing payroll

So how much working capital do you actually need? A rule of thumb is that you have enough money in the bank when you get started to get things going and to feed, clothe, and house you and your family for six months. But a rule of thumb is only that. You can come up with some actual numbers by answering the following three questions and doing the accompanying exercises:

1. How much money do you have?
2. How much money will you need to start your business?
3. How much money will you need to stay in business?

As you calculate these numbers, remember that one of the smartest things you can do is to keep your overhead low. Don't by brand-new office furniture if you do not need to. If you have a computer that works, use that.

How Much Money Do You Have?

Assets		Liabilities	
Cash on hand	_____	Accounts payable	_____
Savings accounts	_____	Notes payable	_____
Stocks and bonds	_____	Contracts	_____
Securities	_____	Taxes	_____
Accounts receivable	_____	Student loans	_____
Real estate	_____	Real estate loans	_____
Life insurance (cash value)	_____	Credit cards	_____
Automobiles	_____	Auto loans	_____
Other assets	_____	Other liabilities	_____
Total Assets	_____	Total Liabilities	_____

Net Worth (Assets minus Liabilities) _____

When you start to turn a profit, then you can indulge a bit. But right now, be conservative. You will be glad you did.

What do you do with all of this information? Begin by multiplying the last number on the expenses worksheet by six. This is the amount of cash you

---

✎ How Much Money Will You Need to Start Your Business?

Furniture	$_____
Computer hardware and software	_____
Services and supplies	_____
Equipment	_____
Beginning inventory costs	_____
Real estate improvements	_____
Legal and accounting fees	_____
Other professional services	_____
Licenses and permits	_____
Telephone and utility deposits	_____
Insurance	_____
Signs	_____
Marketing	_____
Advertising	_____
Labor	_____
Internet	_____
Emergency fund	_____
Other	_____
Total Start-Up Costs:	$_____

✎ How Much Money Will You Need to Stay in Business?

Expenses, per month

Your personal living expenses $_____

Advertising   _____

Marketing   _____

Inventory   _____

Supplies   _____

Utilities   _____

Telephone and Internet   _____

Insurance   _____

Taxes   _____

Maintenance and upkeep   _____

Delivery/transportation   _____

Lease payments   _____

Dues and subscriptions   _____

Debt repayment   _____

Payroll, other than owner   _____

Your salary   _____

Sales tax   _____

Rent or mortgage   _____

Storage and shipping   _____

Transportation and delivery   _____

Miscellaneous   _____

Total Expenses $_____

will need to cover operating expenses for six months, and six months is the minimum amount you will need to get started. You absolutely must have this amount available before opening your business. This money will ensure that you will be able to continue in business during the crucial early stages.

Next, you must add this number to the total in the start-up costs worksheet. By adding the total start-up costs to the total expenses for six months, you can learn what the estimated costs will be to start and operate your business for six months. By subtracting this total from your cash available (the amount in the first worksheet), you can determine the amount of additional financing you will need.

Business Loans

As indicated, because the new business presents a risk to banks, conventional loans are not always easy to get. The U.S. government knows this, yet it wants to encourage entrepreneurship. As a result, the U.S. Small Business Administration (SBA) can be one of the best friends your new business can have.

Although the SBA does not make loans, it guarantees them. A bank might be far more inclined to loan your new business money if the SBA guarantees the loan. The SBA works with about 150 approved lenders nationwide that actually make the loans. The SBA's intermediary lenders have experience making and servicing loans and providing technical assistance to the borrowers. That means that not only can a new business get a loan, but the lenders also can offer business guidance in the process.

The SBA has created many different types of loans that it offers through its member banks. For example, the SBA Microloan Program lends a maximum of $35,000 to entrepreneurs in any stage of business. Other loans go up to $1 million. To learn more about SBA loans and to find a list of intermediary lenders in your area, go to <www.sba.gov>, or call 800-U-ASK-SBA (800-827-5722).

The Four Cs

Whether you work with an SBA lender or not, you will still need to qualify for the loan. While it is basically true that a loan is a loan, lenders have different criteria for making a small business loan. You must understand what the bank is looking for so that you can meet those conditions.

Because an element of risk is involved in every loan a bank makes, your job is to make your bank feel that your loan's risk is low. You can do this if you understand the Four Cs of business banking. A banker that considers a business loan will analyze your loan application through the filter of these Four Cs:

1. *Character.* What is the character and integrity of the borrower? To smaller, independent banks, character means a lot, whereas credit scoring dominates the approval process in many larger banks. If you work with a smaller bank, character can be the critical factor between approval and denial. Because your character is so important in the loan approval process, it cannot be underestimated. Character is determined by your past credit history, payment history, letters of reference, and so on.

2. *Capacity.* What is the ability of your business to repay the loan? When it comes to lending, banks are most concerned with cash flow. Many bankers feel that a small business's cash flow statement is the single most important financial document to consider in a loan request, because in it the bank can see if the borrower has the capacity to repay the loan. Make sure you can show your banker that your cash flow picture will work, even with the principal and interest payments included.

3. *Capital.* How much money are you asking for and is the dollar amount requested justified by your supporting documentation? The more money you ask for, the more people will review your loan and the more scrutiny your request will get. Smaller loans are easier to get. If you are unsure how your capital requirement fits with your proposal and with your banker, then it is a good idea to have a preliminary meeting to talk about this to make sure that your request fits all requirements.

4. *Collateral.* Do you have something to pledge to the bank as a security? A small business can offer many different types of collateral—a mortgage on real estate or inventory and accounts receivable, for example. Collateral makes bankers' jobs easier, helps them sleep, and allows them to say yes to loan requests.

If you need capital, think like a banker and understand these four concepts before you apply.

Other Loan Options

If a conventional loan is out of the question, it might help to know that banks make other sorts of loans as well. This is especially true if your business is already generating some money or if you already have clients or assets. Other loans include:

- *Accounts receivable financing.* This revolving line of credit is based on your accounts receivable. A typical program enables you to borrow a predetermined percentage of accounts receivable, usually 80 percent.
- *Purchase order financing.* Say that you have a purchase order for $50,000 worth of widgets, or you sign a $50,000 contract. Using this method of financing, you can obtain advances on contracts that can be repaid directly by your customer.
- *Fixed asset loans.* These loans are based on fixed assets (such as machinery you own).

Angels

If a bank loan is simply not possible, then consider the angel option. An *angel,* as the name implies, is someone who has extra money and who is willing to take a risk on a new venture. But they do so for a price. What price, you ask? Ah, well that's the rub. You will be asked, in all likelihood, not only to give up a big piece of the pie, but also some control. It is not uncommon to give up 30 percent of your business to an angel, as well as a say in how

■ Where to Find Angel Investors Online

- <www.thecapitalnetwork.com>

- <www.garage.com>

- <www.angellegacy.com>

- <www.angelinvestorsonline.com>

- <www.capital-connection.com>

things are run. Angels want to make a big profit on their investments and understand the high risk of a start-up business. Accordingly, they will ask to see tight budgets and realistic sales goals.

Angels are out there, but you have to look for them. Ask around. Meet with some stockbrokers, real estate firms, and the like to get some names of possible investors. If you are willing to give up some power, equity, and decision making, angels can provide an excellent funding source for the new business.

If finding an angel investor is part of your plan, you will need to prepare your pitch, do your research, contact the angel, and research the deal.

Prepare Your Pitch

An "elevator pitch" is business lingo for a proposal that can be explained in the length of time you might be in an elevator with the investor. Let's say you found your angel and, for whatever reason, you both got in an elevator on the 29th floor of a building. You would have about 30 seconds of uninterrupted time to pitch yourself, the business, and the idea. So your elevator pitch must be intriguing, make sense, be short and powerful, and motivate someone into wanting to schedule a meeting or learn more. Even if you are never in an elevator with a potential investor, a quick pitch will still be necessary when the time comes.

The "pitch" aspect also requires two written components:

1. *The executive summary from your business plan.* As you know, it is a compelling overview of your business venture. This may be the first thing the angel will read about your business and why he or she should invest in it. The executive summary should state clearly how much seed capital you need.
2. *The business plan itself.* If the angel likes the executive summary, he or she will want to see the whole plan.

Do Your Research

By using the online resources listed at the left, you can come up with a list of potential angels and then narrow it down to a few of the most likely. Once you do that, you need to learn about each person.

- Where did they make their money?
- What are their business interests?

- What motivates them?
- What else have they funded?

Contact the Angel

This is when you will need both an oral and written pitch. The important thing is to pique his or her interest and find some common ground. If you were referred to him by someone you both know, tell him. If you are starting a business like the one she started, let her know. Do you like the same ballclub? By creating a sense of common ground with a prospective angel, you increase the chances that your funding proposal will be taken seriously.

> Remember that many angels like being advisors and mentors and may be willing to use their own contacts to help you find additional funding or other assistance. All you have to do is ask.

Research the Deal

If you are offered money, have your lawyer review all agreements. Also, get some references from the angel for other deals he or she has done. Check the references and make sure the angel is good to work with and legitimate.

Venture Capital

Venture capital (VC) is money tapped for large business start-ups—those that need millions of dollars to get going. Venture capitalists pool their money into a joint fund to make these investments. Typically, a venture capitalist will provide early financing to new businesses that show the potential for rapid and profitable growth. In exchange, the venture capital firm will get stock, a say in business matters, and probably a few seats on the board.

> ■ **Where to Find Venture Capital Online**
>
> • <www.usinvestor.com>
>
> • <www.vfinance.com>
>
> • <www.herring.com>
>
> • <www.vcmarketplace.com/vcdirectory.htm>

The Old-Fashioned Way

For many new businesses, loans, angels, and VC money are simply not an option. What then? Here are some other options that are used often to fund the dream:

- *Use your savings.* It is not uncommon for entrepreneurs to have to put dreams off for a while until they have saved enough to get started. Even if you plan on getting an outside investor, he or she will still likely want to see that you have your own money on the line too. You can always cash out your life insurance; whole life policies have a cash value that you can either cash out or borrow against. You also can sell your stocks and bonds.
- *Tap your retirement.* You may have a 401(k) plan or an IRA. Either way, these funds are possible sources of start-up capital. Before you decide to tap these funds, make sure it is legal to do so where you live as each state is different.
- *Use your credit cards.* A common place people get start-up funds from is their credit cards. Although entrepreneurs do this all of the time, be cautious. Interest rates of 18 percent can foster unmanageable debt very quickly.
- *Borrow.* Other people's money has been a source for new businesses for as long as there have been businesses. The first place to look is your friends and family. Maybe your dad would be willing to give you a loan against a future inheritance or you might have a good friend who believes in you.

- *Find a cosigner.* You can always ask another person to sign on a loan in order to augment your credit. But remember that a cosigner also is liable for the note. If you fail to pay it, the bank will go after your cosigner.
- *Use home equity.* Banks are more than happy to lend you money against the equity in your house. Beware, though, because a new business is a risky venture. If it doesn't work and you are unable to repay the loan, not only will you lose your business but you also could lose your home. For this reason, home equity loans are an option of last resort.

THE BOTTOM LINE

To get the money you want, you first need to know how much you will need. After that, you can target various sources, including friends and family, banks, angels, and VCs. No matter who you look to tap to fund your venture, they will want to see that you have a plan for making a profit and paying them back in a timely fashion.

Resources You Can Use

Business Finance.com
<www.businessfinance.com>

Chamberbiz
888-948-1429
1615 H Street, NW, Suite 457
Washington, DC 20062
<www.chamberbiz.com>

The Small Business Administration
409 Third Street, SW
Washington, DC 20416
<www.sba.gov/financing/>

P A R T

III

Opening Up Shop

In this section, you will discover how to create a great business image. Furthermore, vital elements such as business accounting and law are explained in plain English.

10

Creating a Great Image

At the height of the e-commerce boom, an executive from a well-established "old-economy" company was hired to be the new CEO of a young, brash, well-financed Internet start-up. For his first day at his new company, the CEO decided to look his best. He dressed in an expensive suit and his favorite tie. That day, he was to address the company's 100-plus employees. As he tells the story, he felt sharp, and looked great. The new CEO gave an enthusiastic, short introductory speech and then opened the floor to questions. The room was utterly and completely silent. Seconds seemed like hours as people refused to participate. "Come on," he implored, "ask me a question." Finally, someone yelled out, "Why are you wearing a tie?"

As in life, first impressions are awfully important in business too. After someone encounters you and your business for the first time, they will leave with an impression. It may be positive, it may be negative. They may think yours is a well-run, professional enterprise that will provide them with a great service, or not. One thing you can bank on though is that the first impression will very likely be the lens that they use to view your company forever.

Think about it in your own life. If you meet someone for the first time and he acts like a real jerk, don't you label him a jerk? It doesn't matter that he might have been having a bad day. He becomes "the jerk." When you go to a business for the first time and get bad service, don't you usually conclude that their business doesn't deserve your continued patronage? That is why they say that you only have one chance to make a great first impression.

The Importance of a Great Image

Although image isn't everything, it is not insignificant. Your signs, business cards, letterhead, logo, and store/office say much about who you are. Combined, these things constitute your business identity. A professional business identity says that, even though you are new, you are to be taken seriously.

Of course, you will have to back up that great image with great products or services and customer service. But to get people to understand that yours is a business worth patronizing, you have to open the door by having a sharper image. That is the task before you.

Your Logo

A logo is one of the first things you need to create because it will be used on your letterhead, business cards, and other documents. It will distinguish your company, set a tone, and foster your desired image. A logo can be a symbol (the Nike swoosh), a graphic interpretation of your business name (Yahoo!), or both. Either way, it needs to convey the tone of your business. In that sense, it is not unlike naming your business. You want a logo that exemplifies who you are and what it is you do.

When creating a logo, you have two options: you can do it yourself or hire someone to do it for you. If you decide to design your own logo, you will need a software program that offers graphics, clip art, and photographs that can be incorporated into your logo. It is important that you not use any material that is copyrighted in your logo design.

> You can find a great, free logo generator at <www.cooltext.com>.

If you can afford to hire someone to create a logo for you, do it. Prices vary widely; you can expect to pay anywhere from $100 for a graphics student to $10,000 for a seasoned pro. While such high fees can be scary, remember that a good logo can last for 20 years (or more, if you are lucky), which makes a good logo a bargain.

Creating a Business Motto

1. What are the three most distinguishing features of your business?

2. What are the three best benefits customers get by patronizing your business?

3. Make a master list of your best features and benefits.

4. Narrow that list down to the top three features or benefits of your business.

5. Incorporate those into different short, quippy sayings. Be creative. Be wild. Come up with ten different possible mottos based on your features and benefits.

6. Pick the best one.

Also consider making a slogan part of your logo. A good business motto should quickly and memorably convey the essence of your business. And like your logo, your business slogan should be simple and should embody your business. For example:

- Avis: We Try Harder
- Burger King: Have It Your Way
- BMW: The Ultimate Driving Machine

Once you have your logo (or logo and motto), it is time to start putting it on your marketing items—your brochures, business cards, and stationery.

Letterhead and Stationery

For many new businesses, their stationery becomes the most important marketing tool they have. Your stationery is one of your basic links to the outside world (along with your Web site). It is how people will perceive your business. Thus, if you fail to have professional stationery printed and instead simply copy your letterhead and logo onto the top of every document, you will look like an amateur. And a new business can ill afford that.

Stationery need not be boring or expensive. You can get some great ideas about your options, and even order it online at a discount, by visiting these Web sites:

- <www.printglobe.com>

- <www.printingforless.com>

- <http://dir.yahoo.com/Business_and_Economy/Business_to_ Business/Printing/>

Begin with your letterhead. It is as integral to your business identity as your logo and name. What you are looking for is an overall theme for your business that conveys the image you are hoping to create in the mind of consumers. This is done by creating graphic materials that are simpatico with one another, that reinforce each other and your corporate identity. Your letterhead may be the first thing people ever see when looking at your business, so be sure that it is professional. It needs to include the following:

- Name
- Logo
- Address
- Phone number
- Fax number
- E-mail address / Web address

The card stock, font, and color of your stationery are equally important. An off-white linen paper gives a professional image, whereas a fluorescent yellow one gives a festive one. It all depends on what you are looking for and what theme you are trying to create. The graphic artist who helps with a logo can certainly give some good advice here as well.

■   **Elements of Your Image**

These items need to be coordinated and thematic in order to create a dynamic business identity and image:

- Logo

- Stationery

- Business cards

- Brochure

- Signs

- Web site

Business Cards

The same font and stock that you used for your stationery should be used for your business cards as well. In some places in the world, Asia, for example, a business card is given out at almost every meeting and is the single

You can get an idea of what some great, original business cards look like or you can design your own card by visiting these Web sites:

- <www.color-business-cards.com>

- <www.ebusiness-cards.com>

- <www.businesscardsworld.com>

- <www.iprint.com>

most important marketing tool people use. Although you certainly cannot expect to say a lot on that little piece of card stock, how you say it says a lot.

The key to creating a successful card is to have it reinforce your image without being too busy. Keep it simple, use your logo, make sure it is legible, and include only the most important, relevant information. If you want your card to stand out from the crowd, consider the following:

- Use a nontraditional size or shape.
- Use a cartoon, if appropriate.
- Use colored paper.
- Emboss your cards.

Your Brochure

Not every business will need or use a brochure. Even if a brochure is not traditionally part of businesses like yours, it still might be a great way to create a professional image and bring in business. The thing to be wary of is spending money on a brochure if it really does nothing to add to your business. A brochure can be an expensive item and thus not worth the money if you really don't need it.

When creating a brochure, avoid the following:

- *Making it too busy.* Creating a brochure that is so jam-packed with information that it is unpleasing to the eye and difficult to read is a sure way to waste money. It is much better to keep paragraphs short, use white space, use bullets, and keep it simple.
- *Making the cover boring.* Too many businesses think that headlining their brochure with their business name is a sure way to entice people to read more. If you want people to read your brochure, you must catch their attention (usually with some benefit they could get by reading more) and draw them in.

Ask yourself: What is the purpose of this brochure? Is it an introduction to your business, a selling tool, both, or more? Whatever your answer, your brochure needs to reflect the same values, tone, and theme that will be found in your other image-creating materials. Use your logo. Use your colors. Reinforce your desired image with text and graphics that reflect your business image.

Signs

A big, bold, visible sign in the right location(s) can be one of the best tools for creating an image, as well as generating new business. Signs are obviously most used for retail businesses, especially when drop-in traffic is a key element to your business model.

Signs come in many forms, from cheap wood ones to expensive electrical and glass models. The same considerations that are used in your other materials apply here. If you can get the image of each of your materials to reinforce an overall theme, busy people who don't yet know of your business will easily understand what it is you are about if they are met with consistency.

Choosing the right sign especially is an area where professional expertise is useful. How big should the sign be? What should it say? How big should the letters be? Are there zoning restrictions for the type of sign you want? A sign company will help you figure this all out.

Your Web Site

Even if your business has nothing to do with the Internet, you cannot pass up the chance to create an online image. Indeed, a Web site has become a business necessity. Not only is it an inexpensive way to buttress your image and tell people who you are, but it is also an opportunity to sell more, get more customers, make more money, and impress strangers.

And you need not be Amazon.com to be successful. In fact, you probably don't want to be. Your business Web site should, in all likelihood, be a clean, simple, elegant place that does a few things very well. Your home page should explain what your business is and what the Web site is about. It should be simple and easy to load. Inside, your business address and contact information should be easy to find. Features and benefits of working with you should be prominent.

Beyond that, what you do with your site is up to you. You may want to consider having some features that keep people coming back, because the more they come back to your site, the more likely it is they will buy from you. You can offer such things as:

- *Interactivity.* E-commerce interactivity means providing interactive tools that enable potential customers to learn more about your products. It could also mean offering chat rooms, message boards, or newsletters. Streaming video is a possibility.

- *Members only areas.* Some businesses offer members only domains on their Web sites, where they offer access to premium information, tools, and services. Think about AOL for a moment. It is nothing but a huge members only Web site; not a bad model.
- *Content.* On the Internet, content is king. A site without good, arresting, useful, timely content is a site that is probably going nowhere. Think about the sites you like. What is it that draws you there? In all likelihood, good content is near the top of your list.

Even sites that are product oriented can use good content. Dan Harrison is the owner of <www.poolandspa.com>. For Harrison, content makes the difference. When he started his Web site back in 1994, visitors could purchase thousands of spa and pool products and, at the same time, learn what to do if their pool turned cold or their hot tub got moldy.

Articles are written by Harrison and his staff and include "Ask the Pool Guy" and "Ask the Spa Guy" features. Chat rooms and message boards are also available. Harrison must be doing something right; he saw revenues double to more than $2 million in the first half of 2001.

Where do you get your content? You can write it yourself or hire someone to create content for you. Another option is to buy syndicated content. Syndicated columns, news, horoscopes, weather, sports, and comics can be an economical way to go. Consider the following options:

- <www.isyndicate.com>
- <www.alternet.org>
- <www.clarinet.com>

How do you get a good, clean professional site without spending a fortune? You can hire a Web designer, you can do it yourself, or you can go to a one-stop shop. Web designers are expensive for most businesses ($2,500 and up). If you can afford one, great, because they can give you a great look. Web designers can be found in the Yellow Pages or online by looking for one on a search engine.

An excellent source for inexpensive Web site design for small businesses is <www.ahwebdesign.com>.

Unless you are familiar with a Web design program, designing your site yourself is not easy. Not only is it time-consuming, but it can be frustrating and ultimately end with a poor result.

The most cost-effective solution may be to find a one-stop shop that hosts your site and designs it too. Many e-commerce solutions providers make it very easy for you to find a one-stop solution for doing business on the Internet. These new partnerships often combine site hosting, store setup, and credit card processing into a single package specifically designed for small businesses. Many local Internet service providers offer these services, such as:

- <www.bizland.com>
- Yahoo! Store
- <www.webyourbusiness.com>
- <www.earthlink.net>
- <www.valuewcb.net>
- <www.e-builders.net>

However you choose to go, it is essential that your business find its way onto the Web.

THE BOTTOM LINE

Creating an image that people remember is a matter of consistently applying a thematic design to your front-line marketing materials. Everything from your stationery to your business cards and your Web site needs to reinforce the image you want to create.

Resources You Can Use

Guerrilla Marketing: Secrets for Making Big Profits from Your Small Business
by Jay Conrad Levinson (Mariner Books, 1998)
<www.gmarketing.com>

Business Marketing Association
800-664-4BMA
400 North Michigan Avenue, 15th Floor
Chicago, IL 60611 USA
<www.marketing.org>

<www.marketingsource.com>

<www.ahwebdesign.com>

11

Let the Numbers Do the Talking

Business and money are practically one in the same. How much should you charge for your goods or services? Should you extend credit? How do you go about accepting credit cards? Whatever the issue, understanding the financial aspect of business is vital.

Making a Profit

Just how important is selecting the right price? It could mean the difference between success and failure. One of the most important financial concepts you will need to learn in your new business is the computation of profit and how it relates to your pricing structure. The *gross profit* on a product sold or service rendered is computed as the money you brought in from the sale, less the cost of the goods sold. The key is to compute accurately the cost of goods sold, which can be deceptive.

Let's say you are going to run a childcare center. To compute your gross profit, you have to be able to figure out what it costs you to take care of each child. The way you do that is by computing all of your costs and then dividing by the number of kids you have. Costs in this sort of business might include:

- Rent
- Food for the kids
- Utilities

- Office expenses
- Salaries and wages for you and any staff
- Payroll taxes and employee benefits
- Advertising, promotional, and other sales expenses
- Insurance and bonding
- Auto expenses
- Other expenses

Let's say that it costs you $5,000 a month to run the show, and you bring in $8,000 a month. If you have 10 children, then your expenses would be $5,000 divided 10, or $500 per child. Now you know the minimum amount you must charge to make a profit. Because you are charging $800 per child ($800 × 10 children = $8,000), your gross profit per child is $300. Your total gross profit is $3,000.

While your gross profit is a dollar amount, your *gross profit margin* is expressed as a percentage. It is an equally important number to track because it allows you to keep an eye on profitability trends. The gross profit margin is computed as the gross profit divided by sales. In the example above, your gross profit would be $3,000 divided by $8,000, or 38 percent. That's pretty darn good. Any business that makes 38 percent profit is doing something right.

Pricing Your Goods or Service

It should be clear by now that the wrong price can put you out of business fast. Finding that magic number requires careful thought and planning. In the example above, we know that you must charge at least $500 per child to break even. The trick is to come up with a price that gives you a good profit while still attracting customers.

When first opening their doors, many businesspeople have a hard time knowing what to charge for their product or service. But actually, it's not that hard to figure out. If you sell a product, you base your retail price on your wholesale cost. If your base cost for a widget is $5, start there, then account for your overhead, and you are off.

The real trick is figuring out what to charge when you have a service business. One reason it is hard to determine is that new businesspeople mistakenly assume that their value is the same as it was when they were an employee getting paid for 40 hours of work a week. If your boss paid you $20 an hour, maybe that is what you should charge. But that's not right.

■ Real Life Example

Jeff Hawkins is the inventor of the PalmPilot, his second effort at creating a handheld personal digital assistant (PDA). His first attempt was something called the Zoomer. Priced at $700, the device was far too expensive for a mass-market consumer product. Moreover, the Zoomer had a tiny keyboard, and its handwriting-recognition software didn't work right. To make matters even worse, the Zoomer had drivers for printers and fax machines, making it both big and slow. Says Hawkins, "It was the slowest computer ever made by man. It was too big and too expensive." The Zoomer bombed.

Knowing that he had to have a more reasonably priced product to succeed, Hawkins went back to the proverbial drawing board. His new product had to be small, simple, quick, and cheap. Tinkering again and again, Hawkins kept refining his ideas and, with each revision, the new PDA kept getting smaller and less expensive to produce. Finally, less than three months after Hawkins began rethinking the PDA, Palm had a mockup of its new device that would fit in a shirt pocket and run on AAA batteries. Its four core functions were a calendar, an address book, a to-do list, and a memo pad. The PalmPilot would come to market costing less than $300.

First, you simply cannot bill eight hours for your services every day because, even if your business is going well, you still have to hunt for business, handle administrative issues, plan, and so on. This is why you should probably charge your clients more than your last employer paid you.

For example, if you earned $25 an hour as an employee, you probably should charge $50 an hour once you are self-employed. When I worked for a big law firm, they routinely charged the client double what they paid me. That is how they made a profit, and that is how you can too. This might seem hard to do at first, but you can't let your lack of confidence cause you to underprice your services. If the client could do what you do, he wouldn't need you.

Think of it this way: A rental car may cost $50 a day, which works out to $1,500 a month. It is much more than you would pay per month for a car you owned, yet at times you still rent one because you have a need, and the rental company fulfills that need. It is the same when someone hires you.

When you price your personal services, think like a rental car company and charge for the real value of your services.

Cheaper Isn't Always Better

It is equally important to understand that being the cheapest isn't always smart. When you use price as the only barometer for your services, then other more important things get left out of the equation—like quality, personal service, and promptness. McDonald's can emphasize low prices because that is one of its trademarks. But if you are not a McDonald's-type outfit, constantly discounting fees and prices may be a mistake.

The price of a product tells consumers what kind of value and quality to expect before they buy it. A person who can afford a Mercedes or Jaguar doesn't mind the high price because they associate quality and value with the prices of these cars. Often, in a consumer's mind, a higher price connotes high quality, and a low price means poor quality.

You need to ask yourself whether you are trying to increase profit margins or market share. If you are mostly interested in boosting profits rapidly,

 Pricing Your Product or Service

1. Identify your customers. Are they upscale or middle class? Are they looking for a bargain or is quality more important than price?

2. Determine your gross profit threshold. Use the formula in this chapter to calculate how much money you need to charge per item to break even, and go up from there.

3. Be flexible. Trial and error is the key. Maybe you want to offer a volume discount to a potentially lucrative customer. See what works.

4. What is your service worth? Value is critical. If a customer thinks your product delivers benefits worth $15, you can't sell it for $25.

5. Look at the competition. What you charge also must be measured in comparison to the product the customer is already buying. Thus, what your competition charges is vitally important to consider as well.

then you need to go with a higher price. However, if your goal is to build a big company and capture market share, a lower price will help you sell more, longer. Volkswagen sells far more cars than Mercedes, but Mercedes makes more money per car. If you are going for a broad customer base, then you need to figure out, often by trial and error, what price people will consider a bargain, and what price still allows you to make a profit.

Increasing Your Profit Margin

There are two ways for you to improve your profit margin. First, you can increase your prices. Second, you can lower your overhead. Price increases require a careful reading of the competition, your business model, and sup-

---

■ Let the Numbers Do the Talking

If you don't understand the finances of business, and many entrepreneurs actually do not, you are in trouble. Business decisions that are not based, at least in part, on a cold and hard financial analysis are decisions that can easily go wrong.

For example, assume that your business is looking to add a new product line. How do you know if it will work? Such an important decision should not be based on guesswork or hunches. Instead, you have to *let the numbers do the talking*. Knowing how to crunch the numbers—figuring out what it will cost you to launch the new line, how much you can expect to make, and how quickly you can reasonably expect to make it—will make the decision easy for you. Can you afford a new product line? Will your cash flow allow you to afford it? What kind of return on this investment of capital and time can you expect? *Let the numbers do the talking*.

That's what Starbucks does. How does Starbucks know when to open up another store in a neighborhood? They look at existing stores and notice how long customers have to wait to have their order taken and filled and then open another in that area when the wait gets too long. They *let the numbers do the talking*.

That is what you must do. Can you afford that new product line? Well, what do the numbers say? If the numbers are not there, your brainstorm could be a huge mistake. And if you don't know what the numbers are saying, it is time to learn.

ply and demand for the product you are producing. It has to be done with testing and care.

The second way to increase your gross profit margin is to lower your costs. Decreasing the costs of materials or producing the product more efficiently can accomplish this. Look for a less costly supplier. Maybe our child-care center could shop for food and supplies at a discount warehouse market instead of the grocery store. Keeping your overhead low will help keep you in business.

Whether you are starting a service business, a manufacturing outfit, a wholesaling venture, or a retail store, you should always strive to deliver your product or service more efficiently, with less cost, and at a price that gives you the best profit. The name of the game is, after all, making a profit.

Your Customers' Payment Options

The final financial aspect you need to deal with at this point has to do with what forms of payment to accept. This includes the creation of a credit policy and the decision of whether to accept checks and credit cards.

Extending Credit

If you do decide to extend credit to customers, be picky. There are two important aspects to a successful customer credit policy:

1. Limit you risk.
2. Investigate each customer's creditworthiness.

Once a potential customer has completed the application, you need to verify the facts and assess the company's creditworthiness. You do so by calling references and by using a credit reporting agency or a business consulting firm such as Dun & Bradstreet. Also, most industries have associations that trade credit information. Finally, even if the client seems worthy, and even if he or she checks out, trust your gut.

Accepting Credit Cards

Recent research conducted by the Small Business Administration (SBA) shows that accepting credit cards increases the probability that someone will

✎ Credit Application

Your credit application might look like this:

Business name_____ Date_____

Other names of the business _____

Name of owner _____

Type of business _____

Legal structure of the business _____

Business address _____City_____ State_____ Zip_____

Phone no. _____ Fax no. _____

E-mail _____ Social Security No. _____

How long in business _____ Dun & Bradstreet rated _____

Trade references:

Name _____ Address _____ Ph _____

Name _____ Address _____ Ph _____

Name _____ Address _____ Ph _____

Name _____ Address _____ Ph _____

Bank references:

Name _____ Address _____ Ph _____

Name _____ Address _____ Ph _____

Credit line requested $_____

The undersigned authorizes inquiry as to credit information. We further acknowledge that credit privileges, if granted, may be withdrawn at any time.

(Your credit application might also specify the credit terms, consequences of failing to meet them, late fees, and that the customer is responsible for any attorney fees or collection costs incurred at any time.)

buy, as well as increasing how quickly and how much they purchase. Accepting credit cards then is smart business. It gives you the chance to increase sales by enabling customers to make impulse buys even when they don't have cash in their wallets or sufficient funds in their checking accounts. Accepting credit cards can improve your cash flow because, in most cases, you receive the money within a few days instead of when an invoice comes due. Credit cards also provide a guarantee that you will be paid, without the risks involved in accepting personal checks.

While that is the good news, the bad news is that accepting credit cards is not cheap. Some fees you can expect to pay include:

- The discount rate, which is the actual percentage you are charged per transaction. The percentage ranges from 1.5 percent to 3 percent; the higher your sales, the lower your rate.
- Start-up fees
- Equipment costs, depending on whether you decide to lease or purchase a handheld terminal or go electronic
- Monthly fees
- Miscellaneous fees, including a per-transaction communication cost for connection to the processor, a postage fee for sending statements, and a supply fee for charge slips

To accept major credit cards from customers, your business must establish merchant status with each of the credit card companies whose cards you want to accept. The best place to get merchant status is the bank that already has your business. If your bank turns you down (because of poor credit or lack of credit history), ask around for recommendations from other business owners who accept plastic. Look in the Yellow Pages for other businesses in the same category as yours, and call them and ask where they have their merchant accounts.

If banks turn you down, a second option is to consider independent credit card processing companies, which can be found in the Yellow Pages. Independent accounts take longer to set up and start-up fees are usually higher.

Once your business has been approved for credit, you will receive a start-up kit and instructions on how to use the system. You can start with a phone and a simple imprinter that costs less than $30, but you will get a better discount rate (and get your money credited to your account faster) if you process credit card sales electronically. Although it is more expensive initially, purchasing or leasing a terminal that permits you to swipe the customer's card for instant authorization (and immediate crediting of your merchant account) saves you money in the long run.

Accepting Checks

Bounced checks can cut heavily into your profit and yet you need to accept checks to conduct business. How can you avoid bad checks? Following these five rules can make bad checks a very rare occurrence:

1. *Get identification.* Always ask to see the customer's driver's license or a photo identification card.
2. *Be aware.* Evaluate the check carefully. Smudge marks are a red flag of a forged check, as are smooth edges; real checks are perforated either on the top or on the left side of the check.
3. *Do not accept new checks.* A large majority of bad checks are written on new accounts. Do not accept a check that does not have the customer's name preprinted on it.
4. *Wait before refunding money.* Require a five-business-day waiting period to allow checks to clear before cash refunds are paid.
5. *Call in the pros.* You might benefit from the services of a check-verification company. By paying a monthly fee, you can tap into a database of individuals who write bad, stolen, or forged checks.

THE BOTTOM LINE

By setting up some policies with regard to credit cards and checks and by buying the equipment and tools needed to run your business properly, you will free yourself up to concentrate on sales and growth, rather than issues and problems.

Resources You Can Use

Business Finance Magazine
<www.businessfinancemag.com>

Entrepreneur Magazine
<www.entrepreneur.com>

Forbes Magazine
<www.forbes.com>

Inc. Magazine
<www.inc.com>

CHAPTER

12

Law, Taxes, and Insurance

By setting up your business properly from the outset, you are putting in place a foundation that will help ensure your success. Finding a good lawyer and accountant whose opinions you can trust, learning how to hire and fire employees, and getting properly insured are all part of that solid foundation.

Finding Attorneys and Accountants

Lawyers and accountants are critical business advisors for your new business. They can help steer you away from trouble, and get you out of trouble if need be. Lawyers can help with contracts, leases, hiring and firing employees, and a host of other issues. Accountants will help prepare your taxes and can give other helpful financial advice. Combined, these two professionals can become vital advisors.

But this begs the question: Where do you find a good accountant who knows his or her stuff, or a lawyer you can trust? The best way is through a satisfied customer. A referral will tell you far more about a professional than a dozen television ads. So, if you know someone (or know someone who knows someone) who has a business similar to yours, find out how they like their lawyer or CPA. You need to ask the following questions:

- Did the professional get good results? Did the case settle successfully, was the contract beneficial, were taxes reduced? Results are what count.

- Was the lawyer or accountant accessible? Far too many attorneys are hard to reach and don't return phone calls quickly. A call should be returned within 24 hours. That is what you should insist upon.
- Were the fees reasonable? While you need to be conscious of fees when hiring a professional, they are not the most important thing to be concerned about. As in life, you often get what you pay for; the cheapest attorneys and accountants are probably not the best.
- Who does the work? Many lawyers and accountants (especially at big firms) pawn your work off to underpaid, overworked associates. While this helps keep their fees down, you want to make sure that the person you hire is the one doing the work when it counts.

If you can get a referral for a professional who meets these criteria, call him or her and schedule a meeting. As you are looking to start an important long-term relationship, expect to spend a few hours with the lawyer and accountant. Get a feel for his or her personality. Make sure he or she understands your needs. Find out about his or her background. Get some referrals. Certainly, you should not expect to be billed for this meeting, and if you are, it's a bad omen.

 How to Find Exceptional Professional Advice

Barring a referral from a friend or business associate, here are some ways to find good advisors:

- *Call your local bar association.* Almost all cities have an association of local lawyers called a bar association. The lawyers are listed by their areas of specialty and the bar can usually give you the names of some of its members who have a good reputation. As bar associations are nonpartisan, you can rest assured that the recommendation will be trustworthy.

- *Contact the AICPA.* The American Institute of Certified Public Accountants is the premier national association for CPAs in the United States. Visit their site online at <www.aicpa.org>.

You want to find a professional whose judgment you trust, who is smart and sharp, who seems more concerned about helping you than billing you, and with whom you get along. A tall order for sure, but doable.

Hiring Employees

Hiring employees is an art form that gets easier over time. After a while, you will get a sense about who is real and who is show, about which credentials are important and which are not. While good references are important, they shouldn't be dispositive. Most people have positive references.

It is a good policy to have at least two interviews with a potential employee before hiring him or her. By the second interview, you will be able to get a better read of the candidate; they are often more relaxed and themselves during a second interview.

One thing that helps is a list of questions you want to ask every candidate. This will help you compare responses. What sorts of questions should you ask? Steer clear of personal habits and issues that have no bearing on work. The candidate's private life is private and looking into it when it does not relate to employment is illegal. Discovering his or her work habits, punctuality, and eagerness to please is fine. Asking about sexual orientation is not. If you stick to hard facts and employment qualifications you will be fine.

> It is also important to remember that one cannot discriminate in employment for reasons of race, religion, gender, national origin, age, and the like. So questions relating to such issues would not only be irrelevant, they would be asking for trouble.

The New Employee

As you go about making your hire, it is important to understand that in almost every situation employees are considered *at will*. This means they work at the will of the employer and can be let go for any reason, or no reason. The thing business owners must be wary of is creating a situation where an employee's status changes from at will to *just cause*. An employee whose status is "just cause" is an employee who can only be let go when there is a valid cause to let him or her go; for instance, because the employee has stolen something.

What is the difference? An at-will employee is an employee who does not have a written employment contract or who has not been guaranteed employment for a specific period of time. The important thing for the business owner is to be sure you do not make any promises, either expressly (in an employment contract or employee handbook, for example) or implied (telling the employee, "Don't worry, your job here is safe.").

Review all your application forms, offer letters, employment contracts, handbooks, and manuals to ensure they do not contain any promises of job security or employment for a specific or definite period of time. All such documents should contain an at-will employment statement.

■ When Employees Cannot Be Fired

Even when an employee is clearly at will, there are still times when he or she cannot be fired.

- An employee may not be terminated on the basis of his or her status in a protected legal class. That is, you cannot fire employees because you don't like their color, their sex, their ethnic background, or because they are disabled.

- You cannot fire someone in retaliation against an exercise of statutory rights, such as filing a workers' compensation claim.

- You can't terminate someone in retaliation for an exercise of his or her legal duty, such as jury service.

In this litigious society, even when you have valid reasons for firing an at-will employee, plenty of workers are willing to file frivolous suits, claiming discrimination even where none has occurred. To avoid such claims of wrongful termination, you need to develop clear performance standards and communicate them to your employees. Enforce the standards consistently and uniformly.

Many businesses have a performance evaluation policy or a disciplinary policy. These help document problems and prove you have been fair and forthright. Meet with employees regularly and let them know how they are doing. Most important, document everything, both good and bad, in writing. A paper trail can help avoid litigation. The importance of documentation cannot be overstated.

Keep careful records of all events and actions leading to a discharge, including the dates and circumstances behind each action. Include what policies have been violated and what disciplinary action has been taken. Preserve these records, especially regarding termination. By setting clear standards, enforcing them, and documenting problems, terminations can be much less painful.

Your Business and the Law

You don't have to be a lawyer to write a contract. If you can afford to have a lawyer write yours, you should. But if you can't, then you are going to write your own contracts anyway. If you are going to play lawyer, do so correctly.

How do you write your own contract? There are several ways.

- *Draft it yourself.* Although not the best idea, it can be done. The key is to avoid fancy language and just be as clear and concise as you can. For example: ABC Corp. will sell 5,000 widgets to Bob's Home Business. Bob's will pay $1 per widget and the widgets will be delivered no later than May 1.
- *Buy a software program.* There are several software programs that you can buy that will draft contracts for you.
- *Buy preprinted forms.* These are not as easily customized to your needs as software packages. But remember that printed forms can be changed. If there is a clause that you don't like, cross it out and initial it. Have the other party do the same and you now have a custom contract.

When in business, you also need to be concerned about being accused of negligence (in the legal sense). All businesspeople are obliged to perform their duties as would another reasonable, prudent person doing the same job.

This is called the *standard of care*. If a plumber did a repair poorly, that is, below the standard of care, and if that mistake caused someone harm, then that plumber would be legally negligent.

This is true for any business—you must do your job competently. If you don't, and it causes harm, you can be held liable for all resulting injuries. Another example: An accounting firm is hired to do an audit, but mistakenly fails to see that a VP has been embezzling funds, which the VP continues to do. The accounting firm probably would be liable for all embezzlements after the audit because their mistake (not catching the embezzlement) caused further harm (more money embezzled). And if an electrician improperly puts in a new electrical box that causes a fire that burns down the house, it's his or her fault.

The rule is that you must do your job in the same manner as a reasonable and prudent person in the same position. If you don't and it causes harm, you are liable.

Legal Mistakes to Avoid

Businesses make legal mistakes all the time, and while most are fairly benign, others can be disastrous. Knowing which pitfalls to watch out for can make all the difference between business success and business failure. Following are the five most common legal mistakes small businesses make.

1. Not documenting rights and responsibilities. With the excitement and all of the tasks to perform when starting a business, it is easy to not clearly delineate who will do what. Yet that can be a big mistake. Imagine what can happen when you think that you are in charge of day-to-day operations and your partner thinks the same thing. Therefore, founding shareholders or partners should have a written agreement that addresses the following questions:

- How much time and effort is each person expected to contribute?
- Who will do what?
- How much capital will each person contribute?
- What happens if the business needs more capital?
- What happens if one person leaves the business?
- What happens if one person dies?

2. Ignorance of the law. An old legal maxim is "Ignorance of the law is no excuse," and it's true. Not knowing your legal rights and responsibilities can get you deep into hot water. Here is what you need to learn:

- Basic contract rules
- How to avoid being considered negligent
- How to protect your ideas and inventions via copyright, patent, and trademark law
- Basic employer-employee regulations
- The governmental regulation of your industry

3. Not having written agreements. All of your important business agreements should be in writing for several reasons. First, oral agreements are difficult to enforce and sometimes are not enforceable at all. More important, memories fade over time, people change their stories, and people "remember" the agreement differently. Putting it in writing avoids these problems.

4. Starting the business as a sole proprietorship or partnership instead of a limited liability entity. Partners are jointly liable for all debts and obligations in general partnerships, as are sole proprietors. If you start the business as one of those two kinds of entities and the business encounters a legal problem, your personal assets will be at risk. If instead of a sole proprietorship or partnership, you start the business as a corporation, LLC, or limited partnership, you avoid that possibility and thereby greatly reduce your risk.

5. Getting involved in litigation. Litigation fees can actually bankrupt you. Beware the lawsuit!

Taxes

The following are four tax rules all small businesses should know.

1. Deductions. You can deduct all "ordinary and necessary" business expenses from your revenues to reduce your taxable income. Some deductions such as business travel, equipment, salaries, and rent are obvious. Others are not. Don't overlook these potential deductions:

- *Trips that combine business and pleasure.* If more than half your trip is devoted to business, you can deduct the cost of travel, as well as other business-related expenses.
- *Business losses.* Business losses can be deducted against your personal income to reduce your taxes.
- *Purchases financed by business loans or credit cards.* You can deduct such costs this year even if you won't pay off the loans until next year. You can also deduct the interest on the loans themselves.

"The IRS spends God knows how much of your tax money on these toll-free information hot lines staffed by IRS employees, whose idea of a dynamite tax tip is that you should print neatly. If you ask them a real tax question, such as how you can cheat, they're useless."
—Dave Barry

---

2. Employee taxes. If you hire employees, you need to pay, or withhold from their salaries, a variety of taxes, including:

- *Unemployment tax.* Federal and state unemployment taxes must be paid.
- *Withholding.* Social Security (FICA), Medicare, and federal and state income taxes must be withheld from employees pay.
- *Employer matching.* You must match the FICA and Medicare taxes and pay them along with your employees.

3. Quarterly estimated taxes. This area trips up many an entrepreneur. Failure to keep up with your estimated tax bill can create a slew of IRS penalties. You should pay quarterly estimated taxes if you expect your total tax bill in a given year to exceed $500. How much should you pay? By the end of the year, you must pay either 90 percent of the tax you will owe or 100 percent of last year's tax.

4. Sales taxes. Most services are exempt from sales tax, but most products are not. If you do sell a product or service that is subject to sales tax, you must register with your state's tax department. Then you must track your taxable and nontaxable sales and include that information on your sales tax return.

■ Important Tax Consideration

As you begin to create some procedures for dealing with money and taxes, keep these tips in mind:

- You need a separate business checking account, and you need to deposit all money from the business into that account. Money can then be transferred to your personal account. This helps maintain an accurate record of business income for tax purposes.

- Designate one credit card as a business card and use it only for this purpose. The card does not need to be in the business's name. Business credit card interest is 100 percent deductible. Keep all receipts.

- Keep your appointment book or calendar. Notations can provide back-up information for things like business mileage, telephone expenses, and business trips.

- Keep every receipt related to your business.

- Keep all cancelled checks. In the event of an audit, you will be asked to provide them.

- If you have inventory, you need to physically count what is left at least once a year. Inventory removed for personal use cannot be deducted as a business expense.

- Each year by December 31 you need to issue a Form 1099 to anyone to whom you paid $600 or more for business services during the year. But don't wait until then to get their address and Social Security number, both of which must be included on the 1099 form. It is best to get that information when you hire the person.

Audits

Small businesses are audited more often than individuals, and the results are not usually good. In most cases after an audit, the audited business has to pay additional taxes. Although the IRS audits the same number of people as ten years ago, they are recovering more than four times as much money now thanks to superior software.

How then do you avoid an audit? First of all, don't overdeduct. Be careful of listing every single receipt you have, no matter how tangential, as a deduction. Studies have shown that taxpayers who deduct expenses of more than 65 percent of their gross income are often audited. Taxpayers who deduct 50 percent and less of their income as expenses are audited far less often.

Also, be sure to prepare a proper return. Have it typed and filled out in full. A messy return, or one full of cross outs or Wite-Out is suspicious. Moreover, you should try to avoid showing a loss. Losses do happen and they must be reported, but a business that shows a loss several years in a row is a business that should be out of business. If it's not, something's fishy. Finally, be

---

■ The Home Office Deduction

Before you can deduct expenses for using part of your home in a business, you must meet three stringent requirements:

1. You must regularly use part of your home exclusively for a trade or business. As long as you are using part of your home for business on a continuing, rather than haphazard, basis, you qualify.

2. The use must be exclusive. Exclusive means just that—exclusive. If you use the room for any other purpose, as a spare bedroom, for example, you would not qualify for the home office deduction. Any personal, nonbusiness use would disqualify you.

3. Your home must be the principal place for your business, or you must meet patients, clients, or customers there, or you must use a separate structure on your property exclusively for business purposes.

prepared to back up anything you put in your tax return just in case you are audited. Keep every receipt. They can go a long way to getting you out of a jam should an audit arise.

Insurance

Instead of assuming that you know what sort of insurance you need, you should meet with an insurance broker to evaluate your newfound business needs. Brokers represent more than one insurance company, so they can check various policies and companies to find what is right for you.

Here are the major types of coverage that you should consider and discuss with your broker:

- *Health.* One of the big eye-openers when you start your own business is just how expensive personal health insurance is. There are several ways around this. One is by utilizing a federal law called the Consolidated Omnibus Budget Reconciliation Act of 1985 (COBRA). This law allows you to personally continue your employer-sponsored group medical insurance, dental, and prescription drug coverage on an individual basis after you leave. Another way to lower your health care costs is simply by shopping around. Try <www.ehealthinsurance.com>.
- *Business property.* You should seriously consider obtaining business insurance that covers damage or loss to business equipment. You can also obtain more extensive coverage for damage or loss to business inventory and equipment, including loss of earnings, and errors and omissions.
- *Comprehensive general liability (CGL).* CGL insurance can be critical to your financial health. It does two things. First, it covers you for personal injury damage suffered by visitors to your property for business purposes; for example, a customer trips and breaks her leg going up the stairs to your business. CGL insurance can also provide special liability coverage to protect against claims and damages that result from the rendering of services or sale of products. And, should you get sued, CGL is supposed to cover the cost of your legal defense. If you have ever been sued, you do not need to be told that this could save you tens of thousands of dollars.
- *Business interruption.* This covers losses from an inability to conduct business due to fire, flood, or disaster. It also covers reductions in

business revenue while you recover from the disaster by providing funding to meet cash flow obligations such as payroll and loan payments.

- *Malpractice.* This is used by such professionals as doctors and lawyers to cover damages resulting from substandard work. This can also include errors and omissions and product liability insurance.
- *Workers' compensation.* If you are going to have employees, you will be required by your state to carry workers' compensation insurance for work-related injuries to employees.
- *Disability.* Disability insurance covers you when you can't work because you are disabled due to injury.
- *Life.* Why are you going into business for yourself? One reason is because you want to provide a better life for your spouse and children. Well, what happens to that dream if you die? The dream will likely die too. Life insurance keeps the dream alive.

You need not get all of this insurance all at once. In the start-up phase, it is probably impracticable. Instead, you can phase your insurance needs in as your business grows. Here is how you might want to proceed:

- *Business start-up.* As capital is needed to get things going and cash flow is minimal, this is a good time to maximize the use of existing policies. Riders to existing policies may cover equipment. Floaters and endorsements to homeowner and auto policies can provide limited protection for business activities in the home or vehicle. You should also consider declaring one of your vehicles as a business car and adjust its policy to cover business activities. You will have to get health insurance right now, and the sooner you buy life insurance the better. You can always increase the amount of coverage as your business grows.
- *Growth phase.* This is when your business begins to expand and cash flow starts to increase. This might occur in six months, a year, or later. When it does happen, you may want to consider obtaining separate policies for business property and general liability.
- *Long-term stability.* This is when your business is established and successful and you have a pretty good idea what comes in every month and what goes out. Future growth will be more predictable. This is the time to make a long-term assessment of your insurance needs.

THE BOTTOM LINE

Few entrepreneurs like to think about the boring aspects of business such as law, taxes, and insurance. However, failure to address these things may make your life much more difficult down the road. Insurance, good accountants and lawyers, and knowing a thing or two about the law and taxes can sometimes save you from a heap of trouble.

Resources You Can Use

Findlaw
<www.findlaw.com>

IRS
<www.irs.gov>

Nolo Press
Do-It-Yourself Law
Phone: 800-728-3555
Fax: 800-645-0895
950 Parker Street
Berkeley, CA 94710-2524

IV

Business on a Shoestring

In this section, you learn how to start and run a business without spending a lot of money. Bootstrap financing techniques are examined, as are ways to outfit and grow the business on a shoestring

CHAPTER

13

Bootstrap Financing

You may want to start a business but do not have enough money to do so. Are you out of luck? Nope. Actually, it is safe to say that most businesses start with less than optimum funding. According to the Small Business Administration (SBA), 60 percent of all new businesses begin as undercapitalized start-ups. So you are in good company.

But what it will take is hard work, pluck, and a tad of luck. Creating a shoestring business begins with finding the necessary funding (discussed in this chapter), setting up shop and stocking the store for less (Chapter 14), and then getting people in the door without spending a fortune (Chapter 15).

Ten Rules for Bootstrapping a Business

If you are going to bootstrap a business, there are some rules of the road you should know. As you go about getting the money you need to get started, it will help enormously to keep these ten tips in mind.

Rule 1: You don't need a fortune to get started. It would be great if you had enough money, but just because you don't, it doesn't mean that you can't start a business. Real estate is a great example of this principle. By using a 3 percent FHA loan, you could buy a $100,000 duplex apartment house with a $3,000 down payment. That is pretty darn close to nothing. Even without 97 percent of the money needed, you could start a real estate business.

Arnold Goldstein, author of *Starting on a Shoestring* (John Wiley and Sons) started his first business, Discount City, with $120,000 of merchandise, $20,000 of fixtures, and three months of deferred rent, *using only $2,600 of his own money.*

Rule 2: Not all debt is bad debt. This is an adjunct to Rule 1. If you don't have enough money, then it is possible that you may have to incur debt to get going. But not all debt is bad debt. Some debt is good debt when it enables you to get ahead in life—to start a business, buy a home, finance college, etc. Most millionaires start out deeply in debt to finance their dream. Is it ideal? Of course not. But if you can take on some debt and see a way to pay it back through your business, it's not a bad option.

Rule 3: Be frugal. As an employee, you can waste supplies, make long-distance calls, use FedEx, make too many copies, and spend your management budget without a second thought. But as a businessperson on a budget, you will have to learn to be lean and mean.

Rule 4: Invest only in your best ideas. Remember that no business survives unless it is serving a market need. You may have many ideas, but faced with less money than ideal, you cannot afford to make mistakes. You must invest your time, money, and energy in only your best, most profitable ideas.

Rule 5: Do what it takes. If you only are going to have 25 percent of the money that you need to start, then you must be willing to put in the other 75 percent in the form of time and effort. You will have to work harder and smarter than your competitors. You have to be willing to go the extra mile as a bootstrapper.

Rule 6: Look big. You may be starting a business out of your garage with no funds, but no one needs to know that. It is critical to your success that you project the image of a big, professional business. Until the business does get big and have some money, remember these two important words: Fake it!

■ Beware the Credit Card Trap

While you can take out cash advances from your credit cards to start your business, be careful. The credit card trap is easy to fall into but very hard to get out of. You know the trap, don't you? It follows this pattern:

- You charge for things you otherwise cannot afford or take out cash you have no way of paying back.

- You run up balances on cards that charge you 18 percent interest (and up!).

- You pay only the minimum due each month, covering only the interest and service charge each month.

- You get stuck with a debt that never seems to go down.

Here's how to get out of the trap:

- After you have run up your cards, transfer all balances to the card with the lowest interest rate. This can save you a lot of money every month.

- Better yet, apply for a new card with a really low introductory "teaser" rate (e.g., 4.9%) and transfer all of your balances to that card.

- Once the teaser rate is set to expire, call that company and tell them that you will cancel the card unless they extend the rate for another six months. If they don't agree to do so, cancel the card, apply for another new card with a great rate, and transfer the balance again. This balance transfer dance can save you a ton of money.

- Pay off the total balance as soon as possible and always pay more than the minimum.

Rule 7: Be creative. No money to hire that great Web designer? You better buy a book and learn a Web design program. Another option: barter. Another option: hire a student. As a bootstrapper, you have to constantly be on guard for new ideas and new ways to bring in a buck.

Rule 8: You gotta believe! Northwestern University conducted a study of successful shoestring entrepreneurs and discovered that they typically never owned a business before, had no business education, and, of course, didn't have enough money to start but did anyway. In short, they didn't know enough to be afraid.

Rule 9: Have a passion. Wayne Huzienga started very small and eventually created Blockbuster Video, among many other businesses. Says Huzienga, "I don't think we are unique, we're certainly not smarter than the next guy. So the only thing I can think of that we might do a little differently than some people is we work harder and when we focus in on something we are consumed by it. It becomes a passion."

Rule 10: If you take care of your customers, your customers will take care of you. You may not have as much money as the next guy. You may not have ads as big or a fleet of salesmen, but that does not mean you cannot be the best. One of the best ways to be the best is to offer personal, superior service to your customers.

OPM

While it is difficult to start without enough money, it can be done. A far better solution when you don't have enough money to start a business is to get enough money using OPM—other people's money.

Finding people who will be willing to invest in you will take determination; it usually isn't easy. Without collateral, perseverance will be essential. Why? Because lenders and investors are skeptics, and they should be. Too many start-ups fail, so, accordingly, investors would rather put their capital into successful businesses that want to expand or start-ups that have already been partially funded. The unfunded start-up is the riskiest investment of all.

But it is also, potentially, the most lucrative, and you can use that fact to your advantage. If you are willing to share your pie, have a plan that makes economic sense, and are willing to look long and hard, the right investor can be found. It is the possibility of a big return on their investment, coupled with

Providing Great Customer Service

- *Ask your customers what they want and then give it to them.* Survey your clients and customers. Find out what you are doing right and wrong. Change what needs to be changed.

- *Train your employees.* Your employees will not know what is expected of them until you teach them.

- *Empower your employees.* Give employees the room to solve problems on their own. For instance, at Outback Steakhouse the wait staff can offer patrons free drinks, appetizers, or meals when something goes wrong, without asking a manager.

- *Reward your employees.* Employees who make customers happy are making you money. If they are rewarded for a job well done, that behavior will be reinforced.

- *Do more than expected.* Going above and beyond the call of duty endears you to clients. Do so consistently and your business will take off.

the ability to write off a loss on their taxes, that makes the rich investor a viable alternative for the cash-strapped entrepreneur.

The key will be your ability to entice the right person with the right deal. Investors want a high return. Ask them what they want, and give them what they want. Most investors will want to know what you are putting into the venture, aside from your sweat equity. Be honest. If you are donating equipment or material, say so. If you are tapping credit cards, fess up. Your commitment can only help your cause.

The key to winning over an investor or other lender is to look like a pro. Talking big without back-up facts will make you look a fool. Instead, come in looking like a businessman who understands business. You need facts, data, and hard figures that back up your rosy rhetoric. You must know:

- How much you really need
- Why you need that much
- How much you can afford to pay back every month
- How you will make that amount

If you can answer these questions confidently, then it is time to go over your options because there are many ways to finance your business using OPM.

■ Structuring the Deal

When structuring a loan or investment deal, keep these points in mind:

- *How much money do you need?* Ask for more than you need. Either you will be able to negotiate down to the right amount or you will have more than enough to get started. Either way, you win.

- *Who is taking out the loan?* Make sure that it is your company and not you personally. While you may have to give a personal guarantee for the loan, avoid doing so if at all possible.

- *How much interest will you have to pay?* Remember, everything is negotiable.

- *How long is the term?* You need to run some numbers that tell you how much you can afford to repay every month and how long it will take to pay back the loan. The longer the term, the better for you. If you can pay it back sooner, great, if not, you won't default.

- *Is this your only option?* Be picky. If you can get one lender/investor hooked, you can probably get others.

■ Bootstrapping Your Product

Here are three ways to bootstrap your way into new product development:

1. Work on your product at night and over the weekend while keeping your "day job."

2. Get current customers to fund research and development.

3. Get customers who will be using the product to prepay for licenses or royalties.

Option 1: Find a Partner

Often, the best businesses are those that are started by two people of different backgrounds with different skills sets. You may be a marketing genius but know nothing about finances, and you may have a friend who is financially literate but knows nothing about business. Together, you may make a great team. Martha Stewart has a woman she works with named Sharon Patrick, a steady woman who helps run the empire. Martha likes to compare Ms. Patrick to Jeep—solid and dependable. Many entrepreneurs need their own Jeep, yours just happens to be one who has money, that's all.

■ Real Life Example

In 1930, Chester Carlson landed a job in the New York City patent offices of a small electronics company, where he assembled patent applications. Patent applications are extremely long documents, and Carlson's job of duplicating the drawings and specifications was boring and tedious. Frustrated by his day job, and already prone to inventing, Carlson decided that there must be a better way.

He began to study photography, the physics of light, paper treatment, and printing. His research paid off when he stumbled upon photoconductivity—the method in which light affects the electrical conductivity of materials, thereby allowing him to reproduce documents electronically. Hoping to find a corporate sponsor for his invention, or even someone to whom he could sell it, Carlson spent the next few years meeting with and getting turned down by the likes of GE, RCA, and IBM. He had no luck; he was a genius, but not a marketer.

The break Carlson had been hoping for came in 1947 when Joe Wilson, the president of a small photographic company called Haloid and a marketing wiz, came to see the electronphotograhy machine he had read about. After seeing a demonstration, Wilson exclaimed, "Of course, it's got a million miles to go before it will be marketable. But when it does become marketable, we've got to be in the picture!" Wilson and his company eventually pumped $100 million and ten years into the invention before finally turning Carlson's idea into a workable machine. Deciding that "electron photography" and Haloid weren't snazzy enough names, the marketing wizard decided to rename the process and the company Xerox.

Business partners can take many forms. You may be able to find a "silent" partner who merely wants to invest in return for a share of the company, or you may find someone who is interested in becoming an active participant. However, as discussed in Chapter 7, partnerships are fraught with danger, so be careful.

■ How to Find a Partner with Money

- Networking is essential. Put the word out to your lawyer, accountant, and banker that you are looking for a business partner.

- Speak with friends, family, colleagues, and people where you worship. Word of mouth has found many partners.

- Speak also with suppliers and distributors for possible leads.

- People in your line of work who have retired may be interested in being either a working or silent partner.

- Look online. Try <www.businesspartners.net>.

- Advertise. Most classifieds sections of most newspapers have a Capital Needed section. Also look under the Capital Available section.

When looking at potential partners, keep in mind that entrepreneurship is a risk. Your venture may not succeed, so be extra careful about partnering with friends and family members. Owing money to a close friend or family member after a business goes south is not a pleasant experience.

The important thing to remember when looking for a partner is that you will get the money you desire only if the partner gets what he or she wants. Does he want to be involved in day-to-day operations? If so, you better be sure that this is someone with whom you can work. Does she just want a return on her investment? Then you better have a solid financial plan. Ask them what they want and then give them what they want.

Option 2: Distributor and Supplier Financing

Distributors and suppliers want your business. They want you to become a lucrative, repeat customer. As such, they know that one way to do that is to help you get started. If you seem solid and creditworthy, getting a start-up loan from a distributor or supplier is not out of the question.

Given that most industries are very competitive and have numerous suppliers, it may even be possible to negotiate one against the other to see who will offer you the best deal. Your best bet is to focus on the largest suppliers in your field and make a sophisticated, professional pitch to them. Yet, who knows? It may be that a newer, smaller distributor may be more anxious to earn your business and will be more amenable to the pitch. When you are a bootstrapper, you have to be willing to fall down to succeed.

■ How Supplier Financing Works

Before a supplier helps finance your business, it usually will visit your site, research your reputation, contact your bank, and call your references. It will want to be sure you are someone of honesty and integrity.

Again, the key to success is preparation. An idea is not enough. Have a solid presentation ready that explains how your great business plan can benefit the supplier's bottom line. Show the need for your service or product. One of the best things you can do is get some preorders and go back to the supplier and explain that you need financing to fill those orders.

Option 3: Franchisor Financing

Finding a franchisor that will finance 50 percent or more of a franchise is very possible. According to the International Franchising Association, roughly 33 percent of all franchisors offer some type of financing. That means the franchisor will finance at least part (and sometimes all) of the franchisee's investment requirements.

Franchisor loans can be structured a variety of ways. Some offer interest only loans with a balloon payment due in five years. Others offer loans that require no payment at all for the first year. Some franchisors finance every-thing, while others offer loans for the franchise fee only. It all depends upon you and the franchisor, so you have to ask. Another option is that most franchisors work with banks and other lenders with whom they have long-established relations. These preferred lenders may also be able to help. Other franchisor alternatives, aside from direct financing, include loan guarantees or working capital.

Finally, in addition to helping with the start-up costs, many franchisors usually have arrangements with leasing companies for the equipment needed to run the franchise. This can be a major expense, so don't overlook this possibility.

Option 4: Venture Capital Firms and Angel Investors

As discussed in Chapter 9, individuals who have made a lot of money often want to invest it. Venture capital firm investments usually start at $500,000 and go up from there. Angels are hard to generalize, but investments of $50,000 and up is not far off.

The main thing that these sorts of investors look at is the management team of the enterprise. They know that their investment is only as good as the people running the business.

Other things they will look at include:

- The ability to become highly profitable and dominate an industry
- Strong leadership
- Experience, tenacity, commitment, and integrity
- Innovation
- A great product

The Web is the best place to find these sorts of investors. Some sites you might try are:

- <www.1000ventures.com>
- <www.garage.com>
- <www.vcapital.com>
- <www.findingmoney.com>
- <www.capital-connection.com>
- <www.investorguide.com>
- <www.business.com/directory/financial_services/venture_capital/>

Option 5: Seller Financing

A final option for starting a business on a shoestring is to buy an established business and have the seller finance all or part of the purchase. Seller financing is actually quite common in the sale of small businesses. While there are many reasons for this, including lack of bank financing, seller financing is an option because it offers benefits for both the buyer and the seller.

For the buyer, seller financing reduces the risk that the business is successful only because of the present owner's contacts or specialized knowledge. If you wanted to buy a music store for example, there is a possibility some customers may not remain loyal without the long-established owner on the premises. But seller financing alleviates this fear. By having the seller finance part of the purchase price, it tells you that he believes the business can thrive on its own.

From a buyer's perspective, seller financing not only indicates that the seller believes in the business, but it also allows him or her to make a better offer for the business, which is good for the seller.

It is likely that a seller will want the buyer to secure the purchase with some collateral. Just as a bank has the right to foreclose on a home if you default on the mortgage, business owners usually want to be able to "foreclose" on the business if you default. That is a small price to pay though for the chance to buy into an established business.

Seller financing may cost you a bit more, but, overall, it can help both sides and should work out fine as long as both parties do their homework and deliver what is promised.

THE BOTTOM LINE

Reread "Ten Rules for Bootstrapping a Business." The bootstrapping entrepreneur will likely have to work harder, longer, and more creatively if he or she is to get funded. But it can happen. By tapping into OPM, you *can* start a business, even if you have little in the way of capital to contribute.

Resources You Can Use

Light One Candle: A Handbook for Bootstrapping Entrepreneurs
by Michael Richards. (Innovation Press, 1998).

The Shoestring Entrepreneur's Guide to the Best Home-Based Franchises
by Robert Spiegel. (Griffin Trade Paperback, 2000).

Starting on a Shoestring
by Arnold S. Goldstein. (Wiley, 1995).

<www.1000ventures.com>

14

Setting Up Shop at Bargain Prices

There is much to buy when starting a business: fixtures, equipment, supplies, and inventory to name just a few. All of these things cost money; money that you may not have. Even so, using some creative tricks, you too can set up a business on a shoestring.

The Story of Johnny's Antiques

It might help to know the story of John, an antiques lover who started what would become a very successful antiques and collectibles shop without a lot of money in Sacramento, California. From the start, John's motto was "It's all in the buying." John knew that the trick to a successful bootstrapping business was to pay as little as possible for what he needed. Here's how John succeeded:

- His first "store" (if you could call it that), was merely some space that he sublet above a friend's established antique dealership. When people would come into the main store, a large sign would encourage them to continue browsing upstairs at Johnny's Antiques.
- He scowered flea markets and garage sales every weekend, looking for bargains. "It's all in the buying," he would always tell me. If he could buy a good piece at a bargain, he knew he would be able to sell it for a profit.

- He bartered for fixtures and shelving.
- He took almost anything he could on consignment, thereby stocking his shelves almost instantly.
- He advertised in inexpensive, offbeat publications.

Most of all, John had the right attitude: he refused to pay too much, was frugal with his money, and always shopped for better bargains. If you are going to bootstrap your business, you must do the same. Be stingy, don't blow your money on high rent and fixtures, and, overall, keep your overhead low. Adopt the attitude.

Don't Blow Your Dough on Rent

In order to start your business on a budget, every dollar you have must be preserved and spent on only the most necessary items. As rent is often one of the biggest expenses a business has, it follows that you will be better able to start your business if you don't spend a lot of money on rent. If you do not need a high-profile location, don't get one. Start small, pick an inexpensive location, and move on to better digs after you are established. An even better option, as discussed in Chapter 2, is to start your business out of your home, if at all possible.

Another low-cost option is to start your business in a business incubator. The purpose of a business incubator, as the name suggests, is to foster and launch new business ventures and increase chances of success by providing low-cost space, overhead, administrative services, equipment, and expertise. Run as nonprofit organizations, business incubators are usually started and funded by governments, universities, or other groups that are interested in job creation and community economic development. Business incubators began in the 1970s and there now are more than 700 in the United States.

The difference between an incubator and shared space is that those who run incubators are dedicated to helping the businesses housed there succeed through in-house management, as well as financial and business consulting. If you are lucky enough to get your venture housed in a business incubator, be ready to get an informal MBA in the process. You will likely learn more about business than you thought possible.

While all business incubators have the same goal in mind—helping to launch successful businesses—each is unique in its own way because many

■ Real Life Example

Berry Gordy was born in 1929 in a Detroit ghetto, one of eight children. His first business venture was a jazz record shop that went bust before too long. Although music was his love, his need to eat found him working on the assembly line at the Ford Motor Company when he was in his early 20s. In his spare time, Gordy made music. Although he was able to move to New York, and wrote a gold record song ("Lonely Teardrops"), Berry Gordy again found himself in Detroit by the late 1950s.

Gordy had learned that if he was going to succeed in the music business, he would need to produce his own records. He borrowed $700 from his sister and set up a ramshackle recording stuio in downtown Detroit. He named his company Motown Records (for the Motor Town of Detroit), and set about looking for talent.

From the beginning, Gordy knew that he had to watch every penny, but his trick was that he used that to his advantage. He decided to make Motown a "family." The singers, artists, songwriters, and producers all lived together and worked together in that studio, creating a special bond (and saving a lot of money). Before long, Berry Gordy had discovered and signed Smokey Robinson, and soon after that, Diana Ross and the Supremes, Marvin Gaye, and Stevie Wonder.

incubators specialize. In the Silicon Valley, for example, you might find a business incubator that fosters high-tech businesses; in Iowa, the incubator may be farming oriented. It all depends upon the nature of the region and the mission of the particular incubator.

The bad news about business incubators is twofold. First, not all incubators are created equal. Some are more successful at accomplishing their goals than others. Second, even if you are not in the best of incubators, you will nevertheless get spoiled. Subsidized rent, camaraderie, and free help are hard to beat. But because the point of a business incubator is to launch new businesses, you will have to move sooner rather than later in order to make room for the next bootstrapping entrepreneur.

■ **Business Incubator Benefits**

- Reduced rent (on average, business incubators charge 25 to 50 percent less than normal rents)

- Shared services and equipment

- Access to financial and business acumen

- Great contacts

- Legitimacy (which can go a long way when looking to lure investors)

- Low overhead

You can learn more and find out what types of incubators are in your area by contacting the National Business Incubation Association at 614-593-4331, or by going to <www.nbia.org>.

Fixtures and Equipment

You do not need new fixtures or new equipment. Your business may look a bit nicer and cleaner, but when you are on a budget (and often, even when you are not), it simply is not worth the extra expense. Buying used can save you a lot of money, and it's even possible to get these things without paying anything up front by searching in the following places:

- *The Yellow Pages.* You will find several businesses that sell used fixtures and equipment. When companies remodel or go out of business, used equipment stores buy fixtures and equipment and, as they say, pass the savings on to you. These places usually have tons of used furniture, fixtures, display cabinets, and other items that you may need to set up your business.
- *The Internet.* One place to start is eBay, but there are also many other online auction houses, used business furnishings sites, and wholesale distributors that can help you equip your store for a bargain.

- *The classified ads.* Used business equipment is a staple of the classifieds. You may even want to place your own ad under "Equipment Needed." Similarly, the back of trade magazines often have used equipment for sale.
- *Auctions.* Out-of-business companies furnish much of the merchandise commercial auction houses offer. Find some auctions in your area and see if you don't find equipment similar to what you need for less than half of what you would pay for it new.

Beyond bargain prices, it should also help to know that much of this equipment can be financed, thus preserving your precious start-up capital for other needs. Banks can sometimes finance 100 percent of used equipment, using the equipment as the collateral.

Moreover, even if you can't find what you need used, many new fixture manufacturers will finance up to 90 percent of your purchase, which again preserves your capital. The problem with this option, though, is that, like a car, new equipment loses its value quickly, and the finance charges manufacturers offer are sometimes significant.

Another option is to see if your suppliers or manufacturers would be willing to help you purchase the equipment necessary to supply their goods, or at least finance part of the purchase. You can sweeten the pot by offering to let the manufacturer or distributor hold title to the equipment, thus giving them a security interest that protects them financially.

Consider, too, the option of leasing any fixtures or equipment you might need. Chapter 13 can give you some ideas about how to do that.

Stocking the Shelves

If you are starting a retail store on a shoestring, you need to understand two things. First, your shelves must be full of enough inventory to turn a profit from the moment you open your doors; nothing looks worse, or is a better recipe for disaster, than a store without enough merchandise. Second, it is possible to stock those shelves with plenty of products without paying for it all up front.

How much merchandise is enough? Well, it depends on how much product you need to move every day to turn a profit. Your business plan should be the place to turn to find this critical number.

Let's say that you have decided to open a convenience store. For the sake of this example, assume that your rent is $1,000 a month and all other expenses total $4,000 a month. How much merchandise do you need? At the bare minimum, the answer is enough to sell $167 of product every day ($167 × 30 days = $5,010). *Let the numbers do the talking!*

Here's another example. In his great book, *Starting on a Shoestring* (from which several of the ideas in this section come), author Arnold Goldstein explains how he opened his first store, Discount City, with $120,000 worth of merchandise. Goldstein writes that that number did not come out of thin air. He let the numbers do the talking. Here's how he came to that conclusion:

- He wanted to make 25 percent profit, so adding that into what he needed to pay his creditors and other bills, Goldstein concluded that he would need $900,000 in sales the first year.
- He determined that the cost for products that would sell for $900,000 was $675,000, so he knew how much it would cost him to buy his inventory for the whole year.
- He also realized that he would likely turn over his stock 5.5 times in the first year, which meant that his opening day inventory would have to be $120,000.

Thus, he learned that $120,000 worth of product turned over 5.5 times would mean that his inventory costs for the first year would be $675,000; this amount would bring in retail sales of $900,000, with which he could pay everybody what he promised and make 25 percent profit. It's all in the numbers.

So where do you get this merchandise when you don't have a big budget? You have to be willing to look, often long and hard, for suppliers who will give you their products on credit. There are tens of thousands of wholesale product suppliers and distributors vying for a chance to sell their wares in your store. Your mission is to find those that will stock your shelves without requiring an up-front payment for the goods. You do so by having them extend you the goods on credit.

Here's how: When speaking with the different salespeople who will be selling you their company's goods, you must make a great impression. If you are not incorporated, you should be. Have a great business plan, a lawyer, business cards, purchase orders printed with your business name, stationery, a location (this is especially important as the supplier will want to see what you have in mind and how good the location is), a banker, and so on. Anything that gives you legitimacy helps your cause.

The salesperson in turn will try to sell you to the company's credit manager. If you have a decent credit rating and some credit references, the chances that the company may say yes increase dramatically. It might take many suppliers who are willing to give you a small amount of credit to fill the store, but who cares? The idea is to get the shelves stocked, and when you are balancing on a shoestring, you have to do whatever it takes.

It also is not impossible to get one large supplier to supply a great percentage of your initial stock—sometimes even 100 percent of your initial inventory. Hardware suppliers do it for hardware stores, liquor wholesalers do it, as do food wholesalers and clothing manufacturers.

■ Finding a Supplier

- Begin by speaking with people already in the line of business you want to start and find out who their suppliers are. Also, look in trade publications to get additional names. Make a list of every possible prospect.

- Put together a great package that will woo suppliers. It should include your business plan, a picture of the location, letters of reference, contact names of your professional advisors, even tax returns. Explain in your proposal exactly what it is you need, how much credit you are asking for, the terms you want, and how you will be paying it back. You need a package that will make a reasonable supplier conclude that you are likely to become a potential new client who will be buying their goods for many years to come.

- Call up suppliers and make appointments with the salespeople in your area. Present the package to them. Ask them to set up an appointment with their company's credit manager or regional sales manager.

- To sweeten the pot, explain that you will agree to continue to buy from them for the term of the loan (but do not agree to use them exclusively), and agree that the supplier will have a "security interest" in the merchandise. This means that if you default or go bankrupt, they will have first dibs on the property.

The credit terms will vary widely. Some suppliers may offer a five-year term at 20 percent interest, while others may demand that you begin to pay them back within 30 days of receipt ("net 30"). Remember that *everything is negotiable.* If you are at a place where you are haggling over terms, the supplier wants you and sees you as a new profit center. That means that you can negotiate and try to get better terms. Extended credit terms are difficult but not impossible to get. Know, however, that once you get them, you will still have to pay cash (COD) for all replacement inventory.

This entire process—from getting initial suppliers to agree to extend you credit to getting additional inventory and paying back the original inventory—will definitely be a balancing act for a few years, but it does work.

Other Options

Aside from supplier-financed inventory, there are other ways to stock your shelves for less:

- Reread the section on finding discounted fixtures. Classified ads, auctions, and the Internet are all viable options for finding discounted merchandise.
- Another attractive option is the use of consignments. Locate a supplier with too much inventory and offer to take it off his or her hands and sell it in your store on consignment.
- Be creative. Once you adopt the can-do attitude that discounted stock is avaialble for those who go looking for it, countless ideas will arise.

THE BOTTOM LINE

If you have the nerve to start a business on a shoestring, you also have enough to stock it without paying retail. Buying used, buying in bulk, buying out of the classifieds, buying at garage sales—whatever works is what you have to do. It's all in the buying.

Resources You Can Use

Discount Shelving
<www.discountshelving.com/dshelv/>

eBay
<www.ebay.com>

Enterweb
<www.enterweb.org/incubtor.htm>

National Business Incubation Association
740-593-4331
20 East Circle Drive, Suite 190
Athens, OH 45701
<www.nbia.org>

Store Fixtures
<www.storefixtures-online.com>

15

Growing Your Business without Big Bucks

If you are going to succeed in your small business, you must get people in the door, and that usually requires an advertising and marketing budget. The bootstrap start-up thus has a doubly daunting challenge: growing the business and doing so without a lot of money. Tough, yes, but it can be done.

Advertising on a Budget

Advertising is the lifeblood for many businesses, but to be effective, it must be done correctly. This is even more true when yours is a bootstrap business. There is no room for error. Accordingly, the first thing you must do is analyze who your customers are, or who they are likely to be. If you don't know to whom you are selling, you won't know where to advertise in order to reach them. How old are they? Where do they come from? What are they looking for?

Once you have a good idea of whom you are looking to attract with your advertising, you can earmark your ad money much more wisely and specifically. The trick is to find the right media source; that is, the one most frequented by your potential customers.

Chapter 16 delves into this subject more fully and explains all of your various media options. Suffice it to say at this juncture that the important thing to know is that there are many ways to advertise for next to nothing.

Buy unused time or space. If you call a magazine, newspaper, radio, or television outlet near their ad deadline, you may find that they have space they have not yet sold. This is called remnant space (for print media) or time (for the electronic media). Remnant buys are often available at a great discount.

Advertise in less traditional media outlets or at odd times. If your business will cater to teens, for example, buying an ad in a local alternative newspaper is much cheaper than your local daily. This is also true for electronic media. Buying an ad on television or radio is much less expensive if you advertise on smaller stations or in the middle of the night. A radio ad that may cost $250 per minute during peak drive times can be had for $25 late at night, and that just may be when your audience is listening. Similarly, your television dollar can go much further if you advertise on cable stations.

And no matter which media outlet you choose, the trick to getting your ad heard for less is to never agree to buy their going "rate card." Find out what they are asking and offer less. Remember the rule: *Everything is negotiable.* It is quite possible to pay less than the going rate if you walk in with cash and a commitment to pay less.

Get your ad produced more cheaply. You do not need to hire an expensive ad agency to create your ad. Be creative. Find a graphic artist who moonlights or approach a student at an art school to create an ad for you. Be willing to barter.

Use flyers. Flyers can advertise specials, offer discounts, grab attention, and, best of all, be created very inexpensively on your computer.

Use door hangers. Hiring some local kids to distribute door hangers can be an inexpensive yet very effective way to bring in business.

Take out a classified ad. Daily and weekly newspapers, as well as local and national magazines, carry inexpensive classified ads, and the people who read them are often in the mood to buy something. Classified ads need to be clear and simple. It is best to offer only one product or service per ad.

Tap into regional papers. Newspapers and other publications often have regional editions that cost much less to advertise in than the regular edition.

Barter. It is sometimes possible to barter your services for ads in various small media outlets.

Have visitors to your Web site "subscribe." Ask visitors to give you their e-mail address in order to get your content and make sure that you explain that their e-mail addresses will be completely private. After that, send them to a special page on your site to sign up, and be sure to have an ad there for your product.

Place an ad in an e-zine. E-zines, or electronic magazines, allow you to reach hundreds or thousands of targeted readers for free or for a very small fee. E-zines are categorized by subject, almost all are free, and many offer free ads for their subscribers. Inexpensive spots are also usually available at the top of each issue.

Use co-op advertising. Here is a great option that you may not know about. It's called cooperative (co-op) advertising. Co-op advertising is a cost-sharing arrangement between a manufacturer and a retailer wherein the retailer places an ad that is partially paid for by the manufacturer in exchange for the manufacturer's product being mentioned in the ad.

For example, when a convenience store advertises a certain beer, you can bet that the beer company helped pay for the ad. That is co-op advertising. Co op opportunities are available in every medium, from Yellow Page listings to print ads and radio and TV spots. Collectively, manufacturers earmark approximately $25 billion dollars annually to help small businesses stretch their advertising dollars. However, according to the Yellow Pages Publishers Association (YPPA), much of the money goes unused.

To start using co-op advertising, ask your suppliers what co-op programs they offer. Follow their rules carefully to be sure you get reimbursed. Some suppliers require that ads feature only their products, not those of any other supplier; others ask that no competing products be included.

Normally, you will need to pay for the ad and then present proof to the supplier that you mentioned their products. For print ads, just a copy of the ad exactly as it was printed will work. If you buy TV or radio ads, you'll need a copy of the script with station affidavits of dates and times aired. You also will need to document the cost of the advertising, usually with copies of applicable invoices from the publication or station where you ran the ad. Finally, you will need to submit a claim and your documentation.

> ### ■ Get the Most from Co-op Advertising
>
> - If you're preparing your own ads, work with the free advertising professionals available at the media outlet you are using to prepare an ad you think will appeal to the manufacturer. Keep in mind the image the manufacturer presents in its own ads.
>
> - Make sure your company's name stands out in the ad. Your goal is not so much to sell the supplier's product but to get customers into your store.
>
> - If there's no established co-op program, pitch your ad campaign to the vendor anyway.
>
> - Expect vendors to help out. After all, you're bringing them business.
>
> - For more information about co-op opportunities, pick up a copy of the *Co-op Source Directory* (National Register Publishing, 800-521-8110).

Yellow Pages Advertising

Advertising in the Yellow Pages is a proven way to get customers and make money. Almost every home has a copy of the Yellow Pages, and when it is opened, the users are in the mood to buy. Many businesses sincerely believe that they would be unable to keep their doors open without being able to advertise in the Yellow Pages. The downside is that buying an ad in the book can be quite expensive, unless you know what you are doing.

If you decide to take out an ad in the Yellow Pages, there are ways to get a discount. First, a Yellow Pages book not sponsored by the local phone company will offer a substantial discount over the well-established leader. And, even if you decide to go with the leader, you should find that it gives first-time advertisers as much as a 50 percent discount.

Also, a business-to-business phone book is certainly cheaper, as are specialty Yellow Pages geared toward a certain ethnicity or group, such as seniors. Also, do not forget that using a manufacturer's name or product in the ad can allow you to tap into some co-op assistance to help pay for your ad.

Tracking Your Ads

When you are on a tight budget, there is no room for error. There are many things that can affect the outcome of an ad campaign—the weather, the economy, even the news. Ads get stale. Neighborhoods change. Customers' tastes and buying habits change. Given all of that volatility, it is important to keep a close eye on the effectiveness of your advertising. When you do advertise, follow these tips to see if your ads are working:

- Track sales a week before an ad runs, the week it runs, and then the week after to see how the ad is pulling.
- When customers call, ask them where they heard about your business.
- Offer customers a small discount (say, 10 percent) to fill out a simple survey on their attitudes about your advertising.
- Run the same ad in two or three different publications, each with an identifying mark. Have customers bring the ads in for a discount and see which ones do best.

Marketing on a Budget

Less than 50 percent of all businesses in the United States rely on advertising to bring in customers. What do they use instead? Marketing. Marketing is a strategy to get your name known by the public so that when they need a product or service, they think of your business. The great thing about marketing is that there are plenty of cheap ways of getting business without spending a lot of money.

The following cost-effective ideas can definitely increase sales and they need not cost a fortune. The key is to choose the methods that are appropriate for your business, marketplace, and style.

Gift certificates. Gift certificates allow present customers to introduce you to new customers. Even better: Because you get paid up front, they help your cash flow.

Brochures. A good brochure is a great selling tool that allows you to provide plenty of information about your business quickly and inexpensively.

Packaging. The plastic bags that customers leave your store with can be great, cost-effective signs. With your name, address, phone number, and logo on the side, bags can be a valuable marketing tool. The same goes for your mailing labels.

Coupons. This is one of the least expensive ways to develop new business. Offering a discount via a coupon is historically a great way to grab attention and get business. Coupons can be put in invoices or church bulletins, sent using direct mail, or simply handed out or placed on windshields.

Giveaways. A free gift reminds your customer of you and your service. Just about anything can be engraved, imprinted, silk-screened, or embroidered with your company name and phone number—pens, key chains, coffee mugs, refrigerator magnets, baseball caps, paperweights, etc.

Speeches. Depending on your topic and your market, you might want to speak before chambers of commerce, trade associations, parent groups, senior citizens, or other local organizations.

Articles. Write an article for a newspaper or magazine, reprint it, and mail it to your customers and prospects. This positions you as an expert, and is a particularly good way to promote a consulting business.

Word-of-mouth advertising. The best source of repeat business is through happy customers. Make sure that your current customers know how valuable they are to you. Send them a flyer or brochure offering a discount for sending in new business. Give something for free to a loyal customer as a way to say thank you.

Seminars. Free seminars also give you an air of authority and allow you to sell without seeming to be a huckster. If you do hold a seminar, be sure to:

- Schedule the event at a time convenient to most attendees
- Be specific in the ad or invitation about when the event begins and ends, who will be there, and what people will get/learn by attending
- Offer great information

Donations. Donating your product or service to a charitable cause often results in positive exposure.

Samples. Giving potential customers a free sample is an excellent way to attract attention and make a positive impression. And, if your product is too expensive to give away outright, offer a free trial to qualified customers.

Press releases. A well-written press release sent to the right media outlet can generate a free story about you and your business that can be used for sales and be reproduced and used again and again to create credibility.

> To learn more about cheap marketing, pick up *Guerrilla Marketing* by Jay Conrad Levinson (Houghton Mifflin), *High-Impact Marketing on a Low-Impact Budget* by John Kremer (Prima Publishing), or *Start-Up Marketing: An Entrepreneur's Guide* by Philip Nulman (Career Press).

Trade shows. Specialized trade shows allow small business owners to promote, sell, network, and check out the competition in one location. Trade shows come in all shapes and sizes. Would-be entrepreneurs can go to franchise expos, gun enthusiasts to guns shows, antiques collectors to antiques shows, and so on. Almost every industry has trade shows. Trade shows are great for the bootstrap entrepreneur because they pack a lot of potential into a short time and need not cost a lot.

And consider the people who attend trade shows: They are so motivated that they use their time to attend an exposition about a certain topic. Like people who open the Yellow Pages, people who go to trade shows usually are looking to buy something. What's even better is that you get to personally meet hundreds of qualified leads.

To be successful at a trade show, you need a booth that attracts some attention because there are so many booths. That means you need to be creative and put some time in planning your booth before the show.

■ Successful Trade Show Tips

- Early-bird registration deals can reduce exhibition fees by 30 percent. Coexhibiting with others whose target audience is the same as yours can cut costs in half.

- You can create an impressive display with used exhibit materials. Look in the telephone directory under "Display Systems."

- Have a drawing for some free services, offer a small gift to the kids, hold a giveaway, or offer special show prices—something to draw attention to your booth.

- Remember that a trade show is a numbers game. You want to meet as many people as you can. The more you meet, the more potential qualified leads you get. One effective tool is to have a short list of questions to quickly separate serious buyers from the lookers. In any case, get contact information from as many people as you can.

- When you do find a buyer, make sure to have a quiet spot in the back of the booth where you can close a sale.

- Because trade shows pack a lot of opportunity into a few days, the pressure can be intense and the hours long. Be sure you have enough people working the booth and rotate your staff to keep them fresh. You want to bring in upbeat people with stamina.

- Use the show to scout new suppliers, scope out the competition, find new strategic partners, and even shop for other trade show venues.

- Remember that not every sale occurs at the show, so follow-up is important. Find a way to stay in touch with your prospects. Send them a newsletter, brochure, or free estimate.

- After the show, bring your team together and see if you can learn some lessons so you can make the next show even better. Review your marketing strategies and brush up your booth selling skills.

Web Sites on a Budget

One of the greatest things about a Web-based business is that you can open your virtual doors without any inventory in stock. Talk about shoestring business models! You do so by outsourcing what is called *fulfillment.*

A truly effective e-commerce site not only offers product and a shopping cart, but it also is able to take an order and send it to a warehouse to fulfill that order. The great thing is that you can hire a fulfillment warehouse that stocks and owns all of the products; you just become the middleman who takes the orders and sends a message to the warehouse to ship the product.

Using fulfillment services, anyone can go online and sell just about anything without having any inventory at all and no one is the wiser. When customers order a product from you, they are, in reality, ordering from your warehouse partner. The key then is to choose the right warehouse service or fulfillment company to act as your partner. The best way to find a warehouse company is through word of mouth or by checking with your industry's trade association. There are many businesses geared toward e-commerce fulfillment. Among those that you might want to check out are:

- <e-fulfillment.com>
- <fulfillmentplus.net>
- <ifssolutions.com>
- <weship4you.com>

Motivating without Money

Your business is often only as good as your employees. If you want to increase sales, it is imperative that you have an energetic, motivated staff. How do you do that without spending a lot of money? The first thing to realize is that we all work for a variety of reasons, money being only one of them. Your job as an entrepreneur is to realize what other things motivate your employees and tap into those.

Often, what people want out of work depends on their age. If you can understand the various motivating factors of different employees, you will be able to provide incentives for a job well done, and do so without raising salaries. The following details some of these groups and what each may be looking for.

Generation Xers

Generation X, comprised of those born roughly between 1964 and 1981, is a different breed of employee. They like a good salary as much as anyone, but just as important, they want to be in a challenging work environment where they can grow while learning new skills.

For the most part, Generation Xers are independent and dubious. They have entered the workforce knowing that they will have several careers and employers throughout their working lives. What this means for you, the frugal yet inspired entrepreneur, is that you can motivate them by creating a work environment that develops their skills, thereby increasing their future marketability. Offer assignments that challenge them, change their jobs around, give them new and different projects, help them learn new skills.

Not surprisingly, training is greatly appreciated by Gen Xers, as is mentoring and other continuing education techniques. Other rewards that work with this group include:

- Telecommuting
- Gift certificates
- Dinners
- Tickets to sporting and cultural events

Finally, remember that younger employees like to have fun and value a work-life balance. A workplace that demonstrates your support of that can go far and doesn't cost any money at all.

Baby Boomers

Baby boomers, born 1946 through 1964, are now middle-aged, and are thinking about family, money, and retirement. Indeed, many boomers are worried about their financial future. As such, one thing you can do to help motivate them is to offer financial planning, good pensions and benefits, and retirement planning.

You should also consider offering flexible work schedules and different retirement options. A survey by the National Institute on Aging found that nearly 80 percent of boomer employees would prefer a retirement plan that is phased-in, rather than occurring all at once. Given that, use job sharing, flex time, independence, and other similar options as ways to keep these employees loyal.

Training, especially computer training, is much appreciated by this group. Finally, consider offering sabbaticals, either paid or unpaid. The possibility of taking four or six months off work can be a great motivator and, therefore, a very effective way to reinvigorate baby-boomer employees.

Older Employees

Older employees, born 1930 through 1945, usually have had a fairly straightforward career and have worked for only a few employers. At this point in their career, they are risk-averse. One of the best things you can offer them is respect for their experience and their knowledge of your industry. Giving them a more important title may help them work past retirement age, if you want them to, especially if they are offered part-time hours and a flexible schedule.

THE BOTTOM LINE

There are many ways of increasing sales without spending a fortune. Everything from flyers to co-op advertising is available. To succeed, you will need to experiment. Try out a few different options and discover which ones work best for your business. After that, turn it into a successful recipe and do it again and again.

Resources You Can Use

Co-op Advertising Programs Sourcebook
<www.co-opsourcebook.com>

Guerilla Marketing
<www.gmarketing.com>

National Association for Promotional & Advertising Allowances Co-op Advertising
<www.napaa.org>

P A R T

V

Growing Your Business

In this section, you will see how to grow your business using proven advertising and marketing strategies. Moreover, ideas for how to care for employees and customers are also provided.

16

Successful Advertising Strategies

Not advertising is like being alone in a dark room—you know you are there, but no one else does. The whole idea of almost all advertising is to turn on the light and let people know you are there. You have to get the phone to ring or get people to come in the store. Advertising will do that.

Advertising in General

Too often, small business advertising is wasted on a scattershot approach that fails to focus on a company's best prospects—the people who are ready, willing, and able to purchase its product or service. Instead of targeting their advertising to a specific audience, these entrepreneurs target a mass audience in an attempt to reach everybody. Often, they reach nobody.

The way to avoid this unenviable fate is really quite simple. Before anything else, you must define your target market. You have to determine:

- Who are your customers?
- Who are you trying to reach with your ad campaign?
- How old are they?
- What sex are they?
- What do they like to do, watch, and read?
- What do they want from you?
- What catches their eye?

Once you have answered these types of questions, picking the vehicle to deliver your message to that market becomes much easier. If, for example, you are going to open an Interior Design office, advertising on the sports page makes no sense, but advertising in the home and garden section would make a lot of sense. Knowing your audience up front will answer many of your questions and save you from costly mistakes.

Advertising Options

Advertising in the newspaper is a great, inexpensive way to reach a big audience. Newspaper ads can be used to promote a sale, grab attention, or offer specials on your product or service. The downside is that newspapers carry lots of ads, so yours can get lost.

Magazine ads cost more than those in the paper, but magazines stay in the house longer than a newspaper, so the price may be worth it. Magazines are especially good for promoting your image and building your brand. Trade magazines are useful for business-to-business advertising.

Radio can be an inexpensive, high-impact way to reach a specific market. Repetition is essential with radio advertising as studies show that it often takes someone hearing your ad six times before it sinks in.

Television advertising is very effective, but is correspondingly expensive. Car companies know more about how to sell their product than almost anyone, and where do they advertise most? Television. Television advertising works, bottom line. Cable channels are more affordable, but are seen by far fewer people.

Yellow Pages advertising is not cheap, but it delivers people who are ready to buy, now. *Internet* advertising is not expensive, but not all that effective in many cases either. *Outdoor* advertising offers high visibility, and the cost per viewer is relatively low.

Let's look at each of these advertising options in more detail.

Newspapers

Almost every home receives a newspaper and there is something in it for everybody: sports, comics, news, classifieds, food, home and garden, etc. For this reason, you are able to reach your target market fairly specifically by advertising in the right section, and that's the whole idea.

There are many advantages to advertising in the newspaper. Newspaper reading can be deliberate and, as such, ads can be examined closely. Your newspaper ad can contain details that electronic ads miss—things like prices, phone numbers, addresses, and coupons. Another advantage is the large variety of ad sizes newspaper advertising offers. If you have a small advertising budget, you can place a small ad without taking a huge financial risk.

While advertising in the newspaper can be great, it is not without some disadvantages. Newspapers are read only once and are then thrown away. Because a newspaper page is fairly large, small ads can be overlooked, and your ad has to compete with other ads and news articles for attention. And there is no assurance that every person who gets the newspaper will see your ad. They may not read the section in which you advertised, they may skip your page, or they may just gloss over your ad.

Despite the downsides, the benefits of newspaper advertising are usually worth the risk and running an ad in a newspaper can make a lot of sense. How do you do so? Every newspaper has its own sales staff and you are normally given your own sales representative. Befriend this person; a newspaper sales rep can be very helpful. Your rep can help you devise a budget, suggest the best sections and days to run your ad, and even have your ad designed in-house.

The hardest questions usually are what size ad to run, how often to run it, and how much to spend. I suggest starting slow and small, and "test" the ad. Once you see that a small ad works and determine when it works best, then you can roll it out, make it bigger, and legitimately expect bigger results.

> Advertising is sold by column and inch, and you can easily determine the size and cost of your ad by looking in the newspaper. For example, an ad that measures 3 columns across and 5 inches down would be a 15-inch ad. If the inch rate is $50, your ad would cost $750 ($50 × 15 inches).

Keep in mind:

- Newspaper circulation decreases on Saturdays and increases on Sundays, the day the paper is most often read.

- Position is vital, so be sure to specify which section you want your ad to be in. Sometimes there is a charge for exact placement, but it is often worth it.
- If you are running a coupon, ask for an outside position to make the coupon easier to cut out.
- The longer you run the ad, the greater the discount you will get.

Magazines

The great thing about magazines is that they target your market fairly specifically. If your business caters to car enthusiasts, for example, advertising in *Car & Driver* might make a lot of sense. Magazines are also good because, unlike newspapers, they are usually kept around for weeks, thus dramatically increasing the chance for many people to see your ad.

The downside is that magazine advertising is usually fairly expensive, and ads often have to be in color to be noticed, increasing the cost even more. Even so, the right ad in the right magazine has launched many businesses.

Radio

Radio can be a very cost-effective way to advertise your business. As with magazines, it is fairly easy to target your market by advertising on the appropriate show. As there are dozens of stations in most areas catering to dozens of different tastes, your job is to find the station and the show that best attracts your desired demographic.

Once you do that, call the station and make an appointment with a sales representative. He or she will be glad to help you write an ad, and will even produce it for you for little or no cost. The trick with radio advertising is to be clever and grab the listener's attention. Humor, music, and sound effects can all be used to great effect on the radio. Notice which ads grab your attention and model your own ad after that. There is no need to reinvent the wheel.

The important thing to remember with radio ads is that repetition is the key. Repetition is the key. Repetition is the key. Say it enough, and your audience will remember your ad. What is the key? See?

Television

Television is the granddaddy of high-impact advertising. Companies don't spend $1 million a minute for ads on the Super Bowl for no reason. They know that television advertising works. It combines visuals with sound and a fairly captive audience.

Of course, the expense can be daunting. Advertising on a network station is expensive and only makes sense if your business has regional appeal. Cable advertising may be good because you can pick the stations that appeal to your audience. As in radio, call up the stations and speak with a sales rep to get an idea about costs and benefits.

Yellow Pages

Do you want the good news or the bad news first? Let's start with the good news. Advertising in the Yellow Pages is a proven way to get customers

---

■ Yellow Pages Advertising

1. *Get a discount.* Less well-known Yellow Pages in your area offer a substantial discount over the well established leader. New advertisers should also get a substantial discount. (See Chapter 15.)

2. *Consider your category.* There might be several different appropriate sections wherein you can run your ad. Thus, a paralegal service might advertise under "Paralegals," or "Bankruptcies," or "Divorce Services." Figure out a few different categories for your business and see which one has the most ads. The odds are, the largest section is the one that is read the most. Also, consider the option of getting several small ads in more than one category.

3. *Tweak your ad.* Leaf through your phone book. Which ads catch your eye? Try to model your ad after one of those. Also, studies have shown that photographs draw people's attention to an ad, as do outrageous headlines and "white space."

4. *Learn more.* A good book that you might want to read is *Yellow Page Advertising: How to Get the Greatest Return on Your Investment* by Jeffrey Price.

and make money. Almost every home has a copy of the Yellow Pages and when it is opened the users are in the mood to buy. Many businesses sincerely believe that they would be unable to keep their doors open without being able to advertise in the Yellow Pages. The downside of using the Yellow Pages is that buying an ad is expensive—quite expensive.

Should you? Well, it depends. Retail services like electricians and locksmiths would be dumb not to advertise in the phone book, because that is where the majority of people go when they are in the market for these types of services. But even more targeted businesses can benefit from a campaign in the Yellow Pages too. For example, a beekeeper supply store might be the only listing in its category. Where would you look if you were new to the bee business and needed supplies?

Internet

Internet billboard ads and popups were once the rage, but not today. While industry execs swear by them, to most people, they are an annoyance to be clicked off as soon as possible. You had better be quite sure someone is going to read your Internet ad before dropping your money here.

Outdoor

Outdoor ads, billboards, bus stop ads, and transit ads can be a good way to attract attention and get the phone to ring because they can be seen by hundreds of thousands of people each month. According to Market Vision Research, the Florida Lottery found that the most effective way to advertise its product was through the use of billboards. Similarly, according to the U.S. Travel Data Center, nine out of ten automobile travelers in the United States rely on billboards to find gas, food, lodging, and tourist attractions.

Creating a Winning Ad

No matter which option you choose, you still need to create an ad that pulls. Interestingly, all ads, no matter the media, are fairly similar in structure. They all must grab attention and make an offer. One simple way to create a successful ad, whatever the media, is through the tried-and-true AIDA method. This stands for attention, interest, desire, and action. The AIDA formula serves as a good blueprint for creating a winning ad of any type—newspaper, magazine, radio, or television.

Attention

The first thing you have to do is grab their attention. Once you do that, you can get a potential customer interested in what you are selling. If you don't get their attention, they will not receive your message among the distractions of the headline news, sports stories, and other more distinctive ads. You must first hit your prospect between the eyes with a powerful headline. A good headline will grab a customer by the throat, show them the benefit of hearing more, and do so in two or three seconds. When writing your ad, keep in mind the benefits that are most likely to get attention include saving money, saving time, making money, and better health.

Beyond the headline, another way to capture their attention is to use a great visual or photograph. One's eye is naturally drawn to pictures, so incorporating one into your headline can really make a difference.

Interest and Desire

After you have the prospect's attention, you have to make your pitch in the body of the ad. You do that by making the customer a compelling offer and describing as many benefits as possible in simple and interesting terms. Because the product or service must fill a market need to be successful, you must explain how it does that. Your ad must be well written so it clearly explains the benefits to customers and keeps their attention.

Action

Finally, you must ask for the order. Give reasons for the customer to buy now, and make it easy for him or her to do so. This will involve a coupon for mail orders, a toll-free order line, an e-mail address, an online order form, a fax order line, or any other means to make it easy and simple to order. Be sure to take the fear out of the purchase as much as possible by giving guarantees, offering testimonials, and showing how the customer is going to miss out if he doesn't order NOW!

If you follow the AIDA formula, you should find that your ad works, no matter what the medium.

When Good Ads Go Bad

Even if you produce a great ad—one with a catchy headline and motivational copy that spurred their interest and called people to action—it can still sometimes fail. Why? Here are four reasons good ads sometimes fail. Avoid these pitfalls to increase the chances that your ad will succeed.

1. *The ad is in the wrong media.* As indicated earlier, before placing any ad, you must determine if the publication (or TV or radio station) reaches your target audience. No matter how great your ad is, it won't pull if you placed it in the wrong media.
2. *Obstacles exist.* People won't buy from you, no matter how great the ad, if it is hard to do so. If your parking lot is too small, if your phone is always busy, if they get stuck in your voice mail, if it is altogether too hard for potential customers to make a purchase, they will give up and buy from someone else.
3. *The offer is not compelling.* The offer in your ad has to be something that stirs people to action. When an otherwise good ad fails to pull, it may be that you have to sweeten the pot and strengthen the offer to make the ad work.
4. *You aren't advertising often enough.* Repetition is the key. Repetition is the key. People usually have to hear or see an ad several times before they actually notice it and respond. You should expect to run your ad with some frequency before it begins to create significant results.

Advertising and the Law

The last thing to understand about advertising is that there are rules by which you have to play. Advertising is regulated by both federal and state laws, and the general rule is that an ad is unlawful if it tends to mislead, deceive, or contain a false statement.

Here's an example: In Los Angeles, a used-car salesman appeared in a television commercial with a chimpanzee and told viewers they could have one of the cars on his lot for "1,000 bananas!" When an enterprising young man drove up with a trailer of bananas, the dealer refused to sell him the car. The man sued and won.

Consumer lawsuits are one result of deceptive advertising. Federal prosecution is another. The Federal Trade Commission (FTC) is the main federal agency that regulates commercial advertising (although state and local governments also go after businesses that violate advertising rules).

Over the years, the FTC has taken action against many businesses accused of engaging in deceptive advertising. If FTC investigators believe an ad violates the law, it usually uses informal means to bring the violator into voluntary compliance. If that doesn't work, things can get awfully expensive for you. The FTC can issue a cease-and-desist order, bring a civil lawsuit, or require you to run corrective ads admitting that you lied and your earlier ad was deceptive.

You have to be careful what you say in your ads. Here are four rules to keep you safe:

1. *Be accurate.* Make sure your ad is factually correct. "Puffing" is OK (e.g., "We are the best dealer in Northern California!"), but deception is not.

2. *Be honest.* It is fine to compare your goods and services with those of other companies, but when you do, make sure every statement in your ad is accurate. Lying about a competitor can lead to a nasty libel suit.

3. *Beware the word* Free! Yes, *free* is the most powerful word in advertising. I am not telling you not to use it, but I am telling you that when you do use it, what you are advertising as free had better really be free.

4. *Have sufficient quantities on hand.* Most states have laws that require advertisers to stock an advertised product in quantities large enough to meet a reasonable demand (unless the ad says "supplies are limited").

Advertising is one of the best things you can do for your business. You can reap the most benefits when your ads are honest.

Resources You Can Use

Advertising Age **Magazine**

THE BOTTOM LINE

Advertising is usually one of the best things you can do for your business, and you have all sorts of outlets in which you can advertise your business: newspapers, magazines, radio, television, Yellow Pages, the Internet, and outdoor ads. In most of these, using the AIDA formula works: attention, interest, desire, and action.

Advertising World
<advertising.utexas.edu/world/>

Creative Advertising: Ideas and Techniques from the World's Best Campaigns
by Mario Pricken (Thames & Hudson, 2002)

***Entrepreneur* Magazine**

17

Successful Marketing Strategies

Customers do not appear out of nowhere. They must hear of your business before they will ever call you, and that is the purpose of marketing. What is marketing? Essentially, it is anything you do to promote your business, get your name remembered, and generate sales. It encompasses promotions, give-aways, publicity, customer relations, public speaking, signs—anything that keeps your business in the public eye and brings customers in the door.

A Cautionary Tale

When Sarah was in law school, she took a class on how to start a law practice. One day, her instructor invited a local lawyer to come speak to the class. One of the first questions he got from the class was the same one you may be asking yourself: Where do we get clients and customers? "Take out a sheet of paper," he said. "If you are going to make it on your own, you will need at least ten sources of business. Make a list of your ten sources." So they did. Most had a list something like this:

1. Dad
2. Friends of Dad
3. Friends and relatives
4. Work associates

After looking the lists over, the attorney exclaimed, "Wrong! You have to think bigger if you're going to make it in your own business." He explained that number one on their list should be "Everyone I know." Whereas most of the students had lists comprised mainly of friends and associates, the successful lawyer showed them that tapping everyone they knew was but *one* of at least *ten* different sources they would need if they wanted to generate business. Advertising would be another. Networking would be another.

This is a good exercise for anyone starting or running a business, and you should do it now. Make a list of ten sources of business. If you are going to make your business a success, you will need to be creative and come up with *many* different ways to generate sales. Marketing must play a major role in that plan.

The Need for a Marketing Plan

The lawyer's tale above is illustrative because it indicates just how few people really have a comprehensive, methodical, well-thought-out plan for generating sales. And make no mistake about it, whether you are opening a dentist's office, a real estate agency, or a bakery, you will be in sales. How are you going to generate those sales? In which media sources will you advertise and which marketing options will you utilize?

A marketing plan will tell you. A marketing plan is nothing more than your plan of action for bringing in business. It need not be long or complicated, it simply needs to be a blueprint that you believe will work for you and to which you are committed.

Your assignment for the rest of this chapter is to look at the various marketing tools available to you, decide on a few that make sense for you and your business, and commit those to paper, along with any advertising strategies you have decided on. Committing to a marketing and advertising plan of action will keep you focused and on target.

Marketing Tools

There are many different methods that you can use to promote your business as part of your overall marketing plan. Following are many different options from which to choose. Pick a few that seem to match your style and business and add those to your plan.

Marketing and Advertising Plan Analysis

1. Who are you trying to attract?
2. What are their needs?
3. What is it you want to sell them?
4. What do you offer that the competition does not?
5. What are the goals of the campaign?
6. How long will it last?
7. Who will be in charge?
8. What is the budget for the campaign?
9. Which marketing and advertising options can you use?
10. How will you be able to measure success?

Correspondence. Any marketing campaign begins with your letterhead, stationery, business cards, etc. These seemingly insignificant things are actually quite important because they represent you to the outside world. If your letterhead is professional, then you are seen as professional. Use high-quality paper. Include all information, including e-mail and fax numbers. All correspondence must be coordinated. Your fax cover sheet should mirror the letterhead which should mirror your business card.

Newsletters. Physical and virtual newsletters are a great way to share information with both potential and actual clients. Aside from positioning you as an expert, they are inexpensive to create and allow you to contact people without looking like a salesperson.

Tap into the magic words. The two greatest words ever invented for business are *FREE!* and *SALE!* People love to get something for less, almost as much as they love to get something for nothing. If you utilize these two words in your promotion, marketing, and advertising materials, people are sure to notice you.

Contests. A contest can generate interest and free publicity for your business. By giving away your goods or services, you simultaneously present yourself as an expert in this area while drawing people to your business because they love free stuff.

> Spencer's dad owned a discount carpet store, the kind of place where everything was always on sale. Spencer spent many hours with his dad at the store. One day when he was about six and just learning how to read, Spencer said proudly to his mom, "Look mom, I can read! S-A-L-E spells . . . carpet!"

Signs. A big, bold sign in the right location can be a very effective way to bring in new business. Retail businesses swear by good signage. A number of different factors need to be considered when choosing a sign:

- From what distance do you want the sign to be seen?
- Do you want it to be seen at night?
- What kind of weather will it be exposed to?
- How much can you afford to spend? Shop around.
- Can you legally put up the sign you desire? Check the zoning ordinances in your area. If your proposed sign is illegal, you will first need to get a variance from the city.

Telemarketing. You can buy some very specific lists and hire inexpensive telemarketers, even students, to sell your product or services over the phone. Telemarketing can also be used to let current customers know of a sale or other promotion.

Direct mail. Like telemarketers, direct mail merchants can also generate some very specific lists, which you can use to send potential customers a flyer or other info. Direct mail is also a great way to stay in touch with current and former customers and is less impersonal than telemarketing. Here are some tips for making direct mail effective:

- Define your audience. The more specifically you can define who your potential customer is, the more successful your direct mail campaign will be.

- Grab their attention. You have about five seconds to generate interest. Use headlines and highlight benefits, benefits, benefits!
- Use a conversational tone.
- Deliver credibility. Include customer testimonials.
- Provide a strong incentive for the recipient to act.
- Include a guarantee.
- Using a self-addressed reply card can increase your response rate.
- Use postscripts (P.S.). Postscripts almost always get read, and provide an excellent place to make an offer.
- Follow up. Often, several letters are needed to clinch the sale or generate a telephone response.
- Don't expect miracles. A good direct mail campaign generates about a 5 percent response. That means that 95 percent of your mailing will be useless.

Commissioned salespeople. Another way to increase business is by having comissioned salespeople sell your wares to different retail stores. The obvious advantage here is that you don't have to pay the salesperson anything until he or she gets a sale and, even then, payment will come from the proceeds of the sale.

Brochures. When you go into a car showroom to look at a new car, what do you leave with? A brochure. The reason is that a brochure enables a potential customer to practically take your product with them and review it at home.

Magnets. All refrigerators are covered with pictures and magnets these days. If you want people to see the name of your business several times a day, give away free refrigerator magnets. This idea works especially well for neighborhood services and restaurants.

Web sites. Even if you are not planning an e-commerce business, having a promotional Web site can be a great marketing tool. You can put your site address on all of your stationery, so people can check your site out later.

Aside from your own Web site, consider the possibility of expanding your business by selling your wares on eBay or other online malls. I once did a bankruptcy for an antiques dealer. Two years later, I ran into him at the airport. He told me he was on his twice-yearly trip to Europe. Apparently, after

■ Business Web Sites

Anthony Hill started AH Web Design with his cousin Rick Roelen in 2001 <www.ahwebdesign.com>. The company specializes in creating Web sites for small businesses. Although they have been offered the chance to create bigger e-commerce sites, Hill and Roelen turned these companies away, preferring instead to concentrate on their target market—small businesses.

According to Hill, the small business market makes a lot of sense because it is where both the need and the demand for their services are highest. Hill believes that every small business needs to have a Web presence for several reasons:

- It is an affordable and easy way for people to learn about your business and contact you.

- Business cards offer too little information. A Web site allows you to provide much more information, while also allowing you to put your best face forward.

- Even if you don't sell goods on the site, putting your Web address in your advertising can increase sales by promoting your business.

Hill says that the best small business Web sites are "clean and simple." Unlike many big e-commerce sites, Hill believes that a small business Web site should be simple, offer plenty of information, and get right to the point. The cost for a simple site starts around $500 and goes up from there. "Every business needs one," says the master Webmaster.

the bankruptcy, he began to sell his antiques on eBay and his business just took off. eBay works.

Don't discount the eBay phenomenon. The site has over 42 million loyal customers and 500 million page views a month; eBay is set to gross more than $30 billion in sales by 2005.

eBay is also useful as a great place to test market your pricing strategy without making a costly mistake. Will that couch sell for $399? Find out on eBay. Will those shoes fly out the door at $9.95? Selling them on eBay first will help you find out.

Testimonials

Satisfied customers can be your best sales tools as they lend credibility to your business.

Excellence

It costs five times more to create a new client than to retain an existing one. Studies show that each satisfied customer will spread the good word about your business to at least one other person, while an unhappy customer will likely complain to many more than that. Doing great work and offering superior customer service can go a long way toward creating continuing revenue.

Networking

Networking begins with your friends and family. Make sure that they know how much you value new business and appreciate referrals. But don't stop there. Join a networking group. For instance, chambers of commerce sponsor networking events where you can meet and mingle with other business owners, who are, in fact, potential customers. Le Tip International is another great group that usually meets weekly and creates a lot of business opportunities for its members. Networking is particularly critical in local service businesses. For certain types of specialized professional consulting fields, such as attorneys or accounting, networking can make a huge difference.

Publicity and Public Relations

Another important aspect of marketing is the ability to get good press for your company. A newspaper article or television news story about your business is like a free commercial and an endorsement all in one. Even better: You can copy the article or make tapes of the story and use them later in other promotions.

Newspaper editors and television producers have to come up with stories to fill their pages and airwaves—day after day, week after week—and it is not always easy to fill all that space. Therefore, your business, along with your ability to publicize it properly and work cooperatively with the media, can become one of the stories if you do it right.

So just how do you get the press to pay attention to your business? Begin by reading the paper or watching your local news closely and noticing which reporters do stories about small businesses. Then you need to think of a "hook" or angle for the story. Local boy makes good is but one example. If you sponsor a charity event, invent something new, lead your community, or open a new store in a needy neighborhood, the press might just become interested in your story. Come up with a hook.

There are two ways to get a media outlet to pay attention to you: sending out a press release or sending out a press kit. A press release is a one- or two-page article that explains the who, what, where, when, and how of your "news." If an editor or producer agrees that the contents of the press release are indeed newsworthy, they will either assign a reporter to interview you about the story, or possibly just print the press release outright in the paper.

A typical press release may read something like the following.

For Immediate Release

Local Real Estate Agent Wins Prestigious Award

Sam Spurgeon, a local real estate agent specializing in investment property sales, joined Western Realty's President Club last week after selling his 100th duplex.

The President Club is a recognition awarded to only the top 5 percent of Western Realty's sales force. "Sam is an outstanding real estate agent who has been an up-and-comer for some time. We are lucky to have him," said Western Realty's president, Sally Edwards. "With the boom in recent real estate prices and the recent decline in the stock market, buying investment property makes sense right now for the average investor," says Spurgeon.

Spurgeon grew up in the Land Park area, went to Land Park High, and graduated from USC in 1995. He now lives in West Hills.

For more information, contact Sam Spurgeon at:
777-777-7777
sspurgeon5000@aol.com
www.SamsNo1.com

An editor who sees this press release may run most of it in the paper or assign a reporter to cover Sam and the changes in the local real estate market.

If you want your press release to get this sort of attention, follow these tips:

- Find out the name of the reporter who covers the area to which your release relates and fax your release to that specific person. Do not fax it to "newsroom" or "editor."
- Create a catchy headline, but avoid hyperbole.
- Be newsworthy. Why would a reader want to read your story? Have an angle that works and fulfills a need.
- Don't sell.
- Keep it short. Your press release should be no more than 500 words.

Besides press releases sent to the right editor, you might also be able to grab some press attention by sending out a press kit. A press kit is a collection of information about you and your business. It could contain a press release, previous stories about you, background information about your business, frequently asked questions, a resume, or almost anything else you think would pique an editor's interest. The purpose of a press kit is to inspire enough interest in you and your business that media types want to know more.

Press kits are relatively inexpensive ways to get you noticed; they can cost anywhere from a couple of hundred to several thousand dollars to produce. Of course, getting noticed does not guarantee you will get a story, but it is a great start. But just what separates a good press kit from a lousy one? Here are a few tips:

- Focus on substance, not flash. A fancy press kit won't fool anybody if you're all hat and no cattle. Journalists see hundreds of press kits a year. You can make yours stand out by calling attention to your substance, instead of relying on a gimmick.
- Tell a story. Newspapers are in the story-telling business. News people report stories and their audience remembers stories.
- Less is more. Focus on the story, the product or service, or the event you want to highlight.
- Offer testimonials. A few good testimonials lend credibility to your press kit.

An editor's job is to report the news. So your job is to become newsworthy. Always remember that news people are in the news business, not the promotion business, so you must offer yourself, via your press kit or press release, as a community asset, not a huckster capitalist.

Be Prepared!

Whatever marketing avenue you choose, it is important to be ready should your plan work. There are few things more embarrassing, and worse for your business, than being hit by a tornado of new business and not being ready—especially when you asked for it!

This is exactly what happened to "Liberty Pizza" (the name has been changed). A new business, Liberty Pizza sent out a press release touting its pizza as the "best pizza west of the Mississippi!" The local newspaper, having received the press release, decided to send out its food critic. The critic loved the pizza and he wrote a story that ran in the Saturday paper that said that the place made the best New York–style pizza in the area.

That night, Liberty Pizza was deluged with take-out orders and dine-in customers. The average wait time for a pizza that night was 90 minutes. And that was before they ran out of dough. Unprepared for the onslaught that their press release created, Liberty Pizza let a golden opportunity slip away. Customers were mad about the wait, mad when they ran out of dough, and mad at the overextended wait staff. The owner later exclaimed that the restaurant had been "just hammered" by the amount of new business that the story created.

The moral is: Like a Boy Scout, be prepared. If you run out of dough, you can't make any "dough," but if all goes well, be prepared to be hammered by new business!

THE BOTTOM LINE

Create a marketing and advertising plan and follow it. The choice of methods available to grow your business is almost inexhaustible, and many are not expensive to use. By using the power of the press (via a press release or press kit), you can gain business and credibility in one fell swoop.

Resources You Can Use

American Marketing Association
800-AMA-1150 (800-262-1150)
311 South Wacker Drive, Suite 5800
Chicago, IL 60606
<www.marketingpower.com>

The Direct Marketing Association
212-768-7277
1120 Avenue of the Americas
New York, NY 10036-6700
<www.the-dma.org>

Guerilla Marketing Online
<www.gmarketing.com>

18

Caring for Customers and Employees

Advertising and marketing have the same goal in mind: to make the phone ring or bring customers in the door. After that, what happens is up to you. If customers like what they see, if they find great products or service, if they are treated well, they will return. When that happens, you have the most prized of all things: a valued, loyal, returning customer.

According to *Inc.* magazine, it costs five times more to create a new customer than it does to retain a current one. Similarly, there is a rule of thumb that says that 80 percent of your business comes from 20 percent of your customers (the 80/20 rule). The best thing you can do to stay successful in business is make new customers consistent customers by treating them well, giving them exceptional service, and doing what you say you will do when you say you will do it.

By the same token, you also need to care for your employees. Employees are the backbone of your business. If they are happy, your business runs well; if they are not, well, you know. Your job once you get your business up and running (among your many other jobs) is to care for these two constituencies. Take care of your customers and employees, and they will take care of you.

The Three Stages of Customers

Almost every business will have three different types of customers: new customers, existing customers, and exiting customers. You need to know how to handle all three correctly if you want to succeed in business.

Creating new customers is an ongoing process, and it is one of the fun aspects of business. Many entrepreneurs enjoy spending their time figuring out ways to lure in new business. Where many drop the ball, however, is after the initial sale. Flush with success, a new entrepreneur often neglects the new customer after that sale, inadvertently failing to realize that that new customer may become one of the valued 20 percent if treated properly. You turn that new customer into a returning customer by treating him or her well from the start. If you don't, it's the business equivalent of a one-night stand.

Existing customers are one of your most valuable business assets and cannot be taken for granted. They usually make up the bulk of your business, so it is incumbent upon you to nurture that relationship and let those customers know how important they are. Existing customers should be given special services and discounts when appropriate, and should always be shown appreciation for their patronage.

Finally, all business will have customers who are ending their relationship for one reason or another, and even this customer needs special treatment. The ending may just be the natural course of the relationship; for example, a chiropractic patient who is ending his care or a customer who is moving away. Because you never know who they talk to or who they may refer to you, this customer needs to be cared for just as well as the others.

Why do customers leave? Consider these statistics from a Small Business Administration (SBA) survey:

- 4 percent of customers leave a business because they have moved away.
- 5 percent change their purchasing habits.
- 9 percent decide that they like the competition better.
- 14 percent become disenchanted with a company's overall service.
- 68 percent feel unappreciated.

The lesson is clear: Unless you want to lose the bulk of your hard-earned customers, you had better make sure they know that you appreciate their patronage.

As old customers leave, you need to constantly be bringing in new customers to take their place. And as you do that, you need to be converting your new customers into existing, loyal customers. This important cycle of your business cannot be ignored. Old customers *will* leave (because they do), and if there are no new customers coming in to pick up the slack, you will soon be out of business.

> At Carpet World, in Long Beach, California, a huge sign reads "Our Word of Mouth Advertising Starts With *You!*" That is the attitude. Taking care of your customers, all of your customers, and letting them know how much you respect and appreciate them will go far toward keeping your business on top.

What Is Great Customer Service?

While "great customer service" is a mantra we all hear about, few businesses actually incorporate it into their modus operandi. It may be because they have never given it much thought, or because it is simply not a priority, or that the culture of the company may be so hectic that employees feel stressed. Unless you want to be on a never-ending quest for new customers because you have no returning, loyal ones, you had better make customer service a priority.

Furthermore, serving your customers well is also a great way to distinguish your business from the competition. You have to give people a reason to patronize your business—better prices, a better location, better products, or, yes, better service.

The essence of superb customer service is that service becomes one of the guiding principles of your business. You need to put pen to paper, create a policy, and then see that every employee receives and understands it. Also, make sure that it is made a part of the employee manual. For employees to realize how important you take customer service, it must be stressed every day, in many ways.

▪ Great Customer Service

- *Be attentive.* Think like a customer. What do they want from you? What are their needs? The better you can meet those needs, the better your customer service.

- *Make it personal.* Endeavor generally to anticipate the needs of particularly special customers. Offer recommendations and ideas that they might be able to use. Become their partner. Send them a handwritten thank you or other token of your appreciation. They won't forget it.

- *Give them a discount.* A discount on future purchases is a great way to make customers feel special (and remain loyal).

- *Keep them informed.* Costco sends its all-important small business customers a special newsletter every month loaded with information, business tips, ads, and discounts. Can you do something similar?

- *Take personal responsibility.* Make sure customer service representatives act promptly, keep their promises, and follow up. The idea is to have one person accept responsibility for fixing a problem, do more than the client expected, and do so in a positive, helpful way.

- *Go the extra mile.* Infusing your troops with the power to solve basic customer problems without seeking extra authority will not only increase the level of your customer service, but it will simultaneously show your employees how important customer service is to the company.

Helping Employees Help Customers

The California Chamber of Commerce recently conducted a survey of 100 of the most successful small businesses in that big state. One of the questions it asked was this: The real key to business success is:

> ### ■ Real Life Example
>
> "For my whole career in retail, I have stuck by one guiding principle. It's a simple one, and I have repeated it over and over and over, but I'm going to say it again anyway: The secret of successful retailing is to give your customers what they want," said the world's greatest retailer, Sam Walton of Wal-Mart.
>
> Walton certainly knows a thing or two about business success. Bigger than Sears, Kmart, and JCPenney combined, with nearly 4,440 stores, Wal-Mart is the world's number one retailer and employs more than one million people worldwide. Not bad, considering Walton started with a single store in Bentonville, Arkansas (population 3,000).
>
> Sam Walton attributes much of his success to customer service, as exemplified by practicing what he called "aggressive hospitality." Said Walton, "Let's be the most friendly—offer a smile of welcome and assistance to all who do us a favor by entering our stores. Give better service—over and beyond what our customers expect. Why not? Exceed your customers' expectations. If you do, they'll come back over and over again."
>
> This philosophy is also expressed in something Wal-Mart calls the "Sundown Rule." It is one reason the company is well known for its customer service. The Sundown Rule states that employees strive to answer customer requests by sundown on the same day the request is made.

A. Hard work and perseverance
B. Fine products and service
C. Advertising
D. Knowing the fundamentals of business
E. Employees

The overwhelming answer was E, employees.

It is not hard to understand why. Employees do the work. Employees make decisions. Employees are on the front lines. It follows then that if you want to offer great customer service, you have to infuse your employees with that desire, because for many businesses, it is the front-line employees who deal with customers on a daily basis. If you want to be known for having great customer relations, your staff needs to know what is expected of them.

■ Helping Your Employees Help Your Customers

- Support employees who deal with customers every day. Make their jobs easier. If they have what they need, they will be happier and that will translate to the customer. Waiters at Outback Steakhouse, for example, are allowed to offer patrons free food after a problem has arisen.

- Train all employees in customer service. One CEO takes training so seriously that he often teaches the customer service class given to new hires himself. This training should also include phone-courtesy training, which is the first contact many people have with your business.

- Stress communication. Again, those who deal with customer complaints need to know how to solve the problem and need to tell the customer that they will solve it. Make sure they keep the customer up to date and offer a solution in a timely manner.

- Reward a job well done.

- Have a "no tolerance" policy. Never tolerate employees who give poor customer service, no matter how bright they may be. If you begin to stress the importance of increasing the quality of your customer relations and back it up with actions, the message will be received.

- Poll customers frequently to get feedback on how you're doing. Not only do most customers not mind giving feedback, they feel important when they do.

- Stress manners. Customers like hearing "Thank you" or "We're so sorry" or other considerate words, when appropriate.

When problems do arise, the company motto should be: This will be fixed. Always acknowledge a customer complaint as soon as possible. Let the customer know you are sufficiently concerned about the problem and your team is on the job to resolve it.

For example, Nordstrom department store has an enviable reputation for superb customer service. One reason is that customer service is stressed, even as early as the initial hiring interviews. One interviewee tells the story of how she was told by a Nordstrom executive that if a customer brought in a used pair of shoes six months after the sale, Nordstrom would gladly take the shoes back. That the customer is number one at Nordstrom is not hyperbole, it is reality. Says David D. Glass, president and CEO of Wal-Mart, "Outstanding customer service and Nordstrom are synonymous. Their innovative approach has allowed them to find out what the customers want and then do it. Their standards of service are what we all shoot for."

Handling Complaints

Indeed, feedback from your customers, whether positive or negative, is one of the most valuable things your business can get. According to the SBA, most business owners get one to five complaints a week, and most are about billing and pricing. Interestingly, the SBA survey also says 95 percent of dissatisfied customers would do business again with a company if their problems were solved quickly and satisfactorily. Solving the customer's problem is your job, even if you disagree with his or her complaint.

All you need to do is listen. To win back dissatisfied customers, be willing to hear them out instead of being defensive. Then placate angry customers by letting them know you are more than happy to correct the problem to their satisfaction. After listening:

- Ask the customer how he or she would prefer the problem be resolved, and resolve it that way if you can. If a customer wants a refund, give it to him or her, if possible. If you do, you will likely keep a customer.
- If the problem has to do with employees, discover whether the problem is endemic and, if so, root it out.
- Even if you are convinced that your business is not to blame, be humble, express your regret that the customer had a bad experience with your company, and offer something to mollify him or her.

Complaints are good because they help you learn what your business is doing wrong. But feedback need not be negative to be helpful. Soliciting feedback is a valuable way to find out what customers like and dislike about your business, as well as a way to discover what they would change or keep.

By offering a small gift certificate for participating, you can learn a lot of valuable information from your clients, while also getting their addresses that you can add to your mailing list. Another benefit of using customer feedback surveys is that you can get testimonials from them. Once you get their permission, those testimonials can be used in your marketing and promotional materials.

Customer feedback can be one of the best friends your business has.

Caring for Employees

Not only must your customers know they are appreciated, but so should your employees. There are many ways you can run your business. You can be a dictator, a jerk, a facilitator, a cheerleader, or any number of other personalities. The important thing to realize is that the style you choose to use will, in large part, determine the kind of business you create. If your employees learn to loathe you, you can bet it will affect the bottom line, just as it would if they learn to love you.

A trait common to many highly successful businesses is that the owners and managers put a lot of effort into communicating with employees to make sure they are happy and motivated. A simple but highly effective thing you can do to create a positive work environment is to be, like Ronald Reagan, a great communicator. Good communication could be a quarterly "state of the company" report to employees, encouraging them to give suggestions or ask questions, or it could be one-on-one meetings devoted to career goals.

Another thing you can do to create a great work environment is to be sure to properly reward your employees. A large part of making employees happy has to do with compensation. Compensation comes in many forms, the most obvious of which are paychecks, bonuses, profit sharing, and stock options. While the thought of sharing profits with employees may nauseate you, consider that doing so becomes an incentive for them to do well, it improves productivity, and shows your appreciation for a job well done. Less evident rewards can also make a difference too. A gift certificate, a luncheon to honor employees who have made outstanding contributions, or free T-shirts all help boost morale.

"Share your profits with all your Associates, and treat them as partners. In turn, they will treat you as a partner, and together you will all perform beyond your wildest expectations. Remain a corporation and retain control if you like, but behave as a servant leader in a partnership. Encourage your Associates to hold a stake in the company. Offer discounted stock, and grant them stock for their retirement. It's the single best thing we ever did."

—Sam Walton, *Made in America*.

There are many measures for employee satisfaction beyond money. Employees want to be appreciated, and they want a life outside the office. Knowing that happy employees create a happy workplace, and, usually, a more productive and profitable workplace, it is not a bad idea to take the pulse of your staff once or twice a year to see how you are doing.

The things that you want to find out, via a feedback form, private meeting, or some other method, include:

- If the employee feels that he is cared about as a person, not just a cog in the machine
- If the employee feels her work is appreciated and praised
- If he feels that people care what he has to say
- If she likes her job, and what she would change about it
- What he needs to perform his job better (tools, training, equipment, support, etc.)

You will be spending a lot of time at your new business and with your employees. Being a good boss is one of the easiest, and least expensive, ways to ensure the success of your business.

The Mission Statement

Another way to let employess know what is expected of them is to create a mission statement for your business. A mission statement is a very effective business tool because it tells you, your employees, and your customers just what your business is really about and where it is supposed to be headed. Knowing what your mission is also helps you know whether your daily activities and policies, are getting you closer to or further from your goal. Thus, it not only keeps you focused, it also helps employees understand what is expected of them.

Many small businesses have a mission statement prominently displayed somewhere, and employees often pay it lip service. But *great businesses* get their employees to actually buy into that mission and believe in it. When

THE BUSINESS START-UP KIT

employees don't understand what the business is about, or if they are forced to heed to some maxim that they neither buy into nor believe is true, morale suffers. Conversely, when they feel part of something larger, their value increases.

■ Creating a Mission Statement

Your mission can be either personal or for your business. In this exercise, we will create one for your business. It should be between 50 and 400 words. It is your dream, your focus, your purpose. Create a mission statement by answering the following questions:

- What personal values do you want to be embodied in your business?

- What qualities and characteristics should be best exemplified by your business?

- What resources are at your disposal?

- What is your niche?

- What is your grand vision for your business? (Don't be shy!)

- Based on your values, vision, characteristics, and resources, what is the purpose of your business?

- Which of your personal qualities do you want to be infused in the business?

- How can your business best serve your clients, family, employees, and investors?

- How much money do you want to make? What are your markets? Who are your customers? What is your responsibility and commitment to them?

- Are you willing to commit to your mission, your vision, your dream? Are you willing to pay the price, whatever that is?

Based on your answers above, based on your values, dreams, plans, niche, resources, etc., draft a mission statement for your business. Make it large and bold and fantastic; something you believe in with all of your heart. Surrender to your purpose.

Excerpted with permission from the *Speaking Success System* by Burt Dubin, the number one speaking success resource in the world <www.speakingsuccess.com>.

One anonymous writer explains the value of a mission this way:

"By intentionally raising your own expectations of yourself, you create a gap between where you are and where you choose to be. Having created this gap for yourself, everything about you automatically begins working on your behalf to close it. This explains why people with a mission enjoy boundless energy."

Here's an example:

Mission Statement

Steven D. Strauss

My MISSION is to be—and to be recognized as and respected as—

The World's Leading Entrepreneur Expert

In support of my MISSION, I will gather and disseminate the very best hints, tips, ideas, and entrepreneurial strategies. I will offer valuable insights and ideas that enable people to be freer, more independent, wealthier, and happier.

Backing my MISSION, I will create significant books, columns, programs, products, businesses, and speeches for the experienced and amateur entrepreneur alike.

Steven D. Strauss

Mission statements can also be created in conjunction with your employees. The value of doing this is that everyone owns the result. The downside is that you may not like the result. For a new start-up, it is probably best to have the top management create the mission statement, and then help all new employees buy into it from the day they are hired.

Liven Up Your Meetings

The purpose of a meeting is to share information, brainstorm, and work toward accomplishing a goal. But that's not what happens at most meetings, and employees tend to tune out when meetings are confusing, lack focus, or are boring. Bad meetings result in more meetings, lower morale, and decreased productivity.

It need not be so. These tips should produce both better meetings and thus a more efficient business:

- *Keep it short and sweet.* Meetings run into trouble when they are allowed to continue ad nauseam. Of course, some meetings need to be long, but those should be the exception. Most meetings, if they stick to a well-thought-out agenda, can be finished in well under an hour, and a good facilitator should keep the meeting on track and moving forward.
- *Speak plain English.* Jargon and mumbo jumbo waste time and make the meeting pointless.
- *Offer recognition.* Recognize the winners on your team. Take a few minutes to congratulate and thank them for meeting goals, closing deals, and making money. Praise reinforces positive behavior and encourages everyone to do well.
- *Open up your circle.* Bring in people from the real world. Have a customer attend a sales or staff meeting and explain why he or she buys from you. This is a powerful dose of reality.
- *Take action.* It is a good idea to create an action plan at the end of every meeting. The plan will list each task that needs to get done, who will do it, and when it will be completed. The action plan should be distributed to everyone who attended.

If your meeting becomes a way to help your staff make more money instead of a rote rendition of the last meeting, then you just might find that the once-dreaded sales or staff meeting is no longer an unwelcome chore.

Resources You Can Use

Breakthrough Customer Service: Best Practices of Leaders in Customer Support
by Stanley A. Brown (Editor) (John Wiley & Sons, 1998).

THE BOTTOM LINE

Customer service must be your mantra. Customers are hard to get and hard to keep, but you can do so by making exceptional customer service a priority. Exceed their expectations. Offer personal service. Fix problems quickly. And, by the same token, it is important to treat employees well. Whether you like it or not, benefits and profit sharing motivate people to do work better. Finally, a mission statement can guide all of these endeavors.

1001 Ways to Energize Employees
by Bob Nelson (Workman Publishing Company, 1997).

1001 Ways to Reward Employees
by Bob Nelson (Workman Publishing Company, 1994).

Raving Fans: A Revolutionary Approach to Customer Service
by Kenneth H. Blanchard (William Morrow & Co., May 1993).

301 Great Customer Service Ideas: From America's Most Innovative Small Companies
by Nancy Artz (Inc. Pub, 1997).

VI

Success Strategies

In this section, important success strategies are examined, from learning how to see business opportunities inherent in challenges to success secrets of the great entrepreneurs—it's all here.

19

Business Jujitsu

Business challenges come in all forms and sizes. It may be a cash crunch that you are unprepared for or losing a huge account. While it is impossible to predict what sort of challenges you will face in your business—and you will face challenges—it is possible to give you some advice about how to prevent the preventable ones.

Business Jujitsu

A new business must have a plan, but it must also be adaptable to an ever-changing marketplace. One thing most new businesses have in common is that they may not have the experience of another more well-established company. This means that you, the new businessperson, need to prove yourself to potential clients. Businesses that have been around the block a few times have established customers and practices. Your task seems more difficult, but it doesn't have to be. Turning a perceived business problem around is not only possible, it also is smart.

Think about it. Yours is a new business. That can be seen as a disadvantage but, seen in the right light, it can also be a tremendous advantage. Your job is to show potential clients and customers that being new is far more an asset than a liability. For example, you could explain to potential clients that because you are new:

- They will get better, more personal service. Because you will have fewer customers as you begin your business, you will be better able to give new customers your time and energy.
- You are hungrier and more eager to please than more well-established companies. New customers will reap the benefits of your desire to prove yourself, do a great job, and establish your business.
- Because you are new, you will cost less than the competition. (If this is not true, it should be.)

If you use your noggin, you should see that any perceived liability can be turned into an asset, because it is just that—a perception. For example, let's say that you are a man who wants to open a ballet school. Sure, that is a traditionally female business. You may stand out like a sore thumb—and that's just what you want! The very difference that your business embodies is exactly what can set it apart, make it distinctive, and really help it to take off. Think smart and any perceived business shortcoming can be turned to your advantage.

Here's a famous example: In 1984, Ronald Reagan was running for re-election against a younger Walter Mondale. At the first of their presidential debates, Reagan looked and sounded like a doddering old man. The buzz was that if he didn't do dramatically better the second time around, he might lose the election. When it was time for the second debate, everyone was watching the 72-year-old president closely. Soon after the debate began, Reagan took the initiative and broached the subject. He acknowledged that age was an issue in the campaign and then, straightfaced, promised not to "exploit, for political purposes, my opponent's youth and inexperience." With that quip, Reagan turned his disadvantage into an advantage, the issue never again came up, and he walked off with the election.

That is what you have to do. If you are able to turn your "liabilities" into assets, you are halfway to entrepreneurial success.

If you think about it, this form of business jujitsu can be used to handle almost any problem you face. The basic idea behind jujitsu is to use an opponent's own weight and strength against him. By turning the tables on an opponent—using leverage, balance, and motion—the jujitsu master can overpower superior opponents. In that sense, one's problem might become an opportunity.

In the area of business, this translates into an attitude. Just as a new business can turn a perceived business disadvantage into an advantage, so too can almost any business turn a business problem around by endeavoring to see it as an opportunity more than an obstacle. But don't think that I am saying that all you need is to have a positive mental attitude, because I am not. Rather, business jujitsu is an attitude that you can adopt to turn almost any business problem into a unique opportunity.

Here are some examples:

- Let's say that you can only afford rent in a low-income area. The business jujitsu master can use this to his advantage by viewing the local residents as another possible client base or profit center.
- Let's say that you are a lawyer and the legislature just radically changed the law in your area of expertise. The business jujitsu master can learn the new law as quickly as possible and then go teach it to other lawyers, making even more money than before.
- Let's say that your main distributor just went out of business. The business jujitsu master can see this as an opportunity to infuse his store with some new products.

Business jujitsu is an attitude that you can adopt that will help you through tough times. Part strategy, part mental trick, part ancient plan of attack, it can keep you one step ahead.

When Bad Things Happen to Good Companies

Something bad will happen to your business, you can count on it. While reading books like this can lessen the likelihood and impact of those unfortunate occurrences, it can prevent them from happening. That is the nature of life, and of business. You can bet that Microsoft, probably the most successful company in the last quarter-century, was ill-prepared for a lawsuit by the Justice Department that accused it of being a monopoly that needs to be broken up. Similarly,

- Firestone never expected that its tires would disintegrate.
- Tylenol never expected that someone would poison its product, nearly destroying the brand.
- Cantor Fitzgerald never could have anticipated that it would lose two-thirds of its 1,000 employees in the World Trade Center attack.
- Pets.com and Webvan didn't expect the dot-com bubble to burst as quickly as it did, putting such well-funded start-ups as these out of business.

So something bad is going to happen; that is not the question. The question is: What are you going to do when it does? Business jujitsu allows you to turn it around so that you are not overwhelmed by it and you see the possibility in it.

The first thing you can do is to be prepared, to the extent possible. You can never know what will be coming down the pike, but the more you know about business and the more you learn, the better prepared you will be when the time comes to handle a problem.

The first thing you can do to prepare your business to handle the inevitable challenge is to read more, take classes, go to seminars, listen to business tapes, and otherwise continue your business education. Knowledge is a very useful and valuable asset to lean on when problems arise.

■ Real Life Example

In El Segundo, California, Marium Industries (name changed to protect privacy) was rocked when a colleague was shot and killed by his wife while he was at work. That the man was much loved and admired in the company made the situation that much worse. "The first thing you must do is ensure the physical safety of your employees. After that, you must look after their emotional well-being. Business must come last," said Hunter Marium, president of of the company.

Marium took the lead as the crisis unfolded, and then helped comfort those traumatized by the incident. He brought in grief counselors, gave people extra time off, and patiently prodded the business back toward normalcy after it was all over.

Mr. Marium's role illustrates that in a time of crisis a business leader must lead. Says Marium, "A crisis is not the time to retreat behind the office door, but rather, the time to be most visible. You must be strong and empathetic. You must communicate clearly and without fear."

A business crisis can take many forms, including:

- Financial (losing customers, theft, a money crunch)
- Violence (terrorism, war, armed robbery)
- Accidents (customers, the public, or employees get injured)

- Products (bad lots, recalls, negative publicity)
- Natural (earthquakes, floods, tornadoes)

Kim Polese was the chairman of Marimba, a software company that had a Manhattan office near the World Trade Center, on September 11, 2001. She was in New York that day about to attend a meeting at the World Trade Center when the attacks came. She never expected that her business crisis would take that form. What Polese discovered was that a business in crisis requires that the president or CEO be strong and available. "The role of the CEO is really being a rock, a source of emotional stability," Polese said.

When a business leader is faced with a crisis, the lessons are clear: Be empathetic, be strong, care for your people, and tell the truth. After that, the best thing you can do is to get everything back to normal as soon as possible. What people want in a time of crisis is some familiarity—a feeling that things can be regular again. You are the one who can lead them there.

■ Handling the Media During a Crisis

- Get a spokesman out there quickly to get out your side of the story.

- Set up a central command post.

- Be honest, credible, forthcoming, direct, and sympathetic.

- Remain calm and courteous.

- Use your Web site to release information.

- Don't speak in jargon; use plain English.

- Avoid saying "No comment."

- Do not speculate. Stick to the facts.

- Avoid discussing fault.

- The media loves a crisis. Resolve it as quickly as possible and let them move on to something else.

Avoiding Common Mistakes

Beyond those moments of crisis, if you are going to survive and be a long-term business success then you need to be aware of the most common mistakes and pitfalls that can ruin the best-laid plans. Business jujitsu requires preparation. The following are potential problems of which to be aware.

Insufficient start-up capital. This is a real killer. You can have the best plan in the world, but if you don't have enough money to get it off the ground and survive for those first few scary months, you are wasting your time and money. Don't start a company if you cannot come up with more capital than you think you'll need—at least enough money to cover the first year, and preferably the second year as well.

Going first class from the start. This is the opposite of the insufficient funds crisis. Until you know what you are doing and until you know how to turn a consistent profit, you need to conserve your funds, no matter how much money you have to start. Dropping $20,000 on an office remodel, new furniture, and a top-of-the-line computer is a prescription for failure. It is analogous to throwing a graduation party for yourself in the first semester of your freshman year. Smart entrepreneurs part with their capital only when they are convinced it will make a real difference.

Failure to analyze the business objectively. Failure to do adequate market research, including getting out into the marketplace and talking to potential customers, is an easily avoidable mistake. You must decide whether there really is a market for your business. Many entrepreneurs have failed because their projections were far too rosy and not grounded in reality. Being optimistic is great, but not at the expense of sound business judgment.

Litigation imbroglio. Lawsuits are legalized war. And they are a danger to the financial well-being of your new start-up. Prosecuting a suit can cost a fortune, as can getting hit with a judgment. Either way, you lose. Justice is all too often not realized. The vast majority of the time, entrepreneurs would be better served by biting their tongues, settling out of court, and getting on with building their businesses.

■ Real Life Example

In the 1980s, Coca-Cola was having some serious problems, despite being one of the biggest, most recognized, companies in the world. At the time, its biggest rival, Pepsi, had begun touting the Pepsi Challenge—a head-to-head taste test whereby cola drinkers were asked to compare the tastes of the two colas. Of course, the television ads always showed Pepsi winning the taste test, but even more troubling to Coca-Cola was that the test results were real. In blind taste tests in the lab, consumers thought Pepsi tested better than Coke. Coke was losing market share, and the company was scared.

So, in what may be the dumbest decision in the history of dumb business decisions, Coca-Cola decided to mess with the greatest brand in history and create what would become an unmitigated disaster, New Coke. Changing the taste of Coke was a radical idea. They might as well have banned moms and outlawed apple pie while they were at it. Nevertheless, on April 23, 1985, New Coke was released to a great deal of fanfare. The reaction to New Coke was swift and strong. People hated it. The Coca-Cola Company suddenly became something of a national joke.

How did this happen? Coca-Cola failed in the most basic business fundamental—it didn't analyze the business properly. Amazingly, Coca-Cola did no test marketing; it never actually tried out the new formula in a few cities to see how people would react to it. Even worse, it never explained to people that liking New Coke meant that there would be no old Coke. A big mistake and a waste of its $4 million worth of research.

Not giving the customer a reason to change. I've said it before, but it bears repeating: You have to give your potential buyers a great reason to consider purchasing your product—better prices, better service, something that distinguishes you. If the buyer has no reason to switch to you, he or she probably won't.

Betting the ranch. As has been stated time and again throughout this book, great entrepreneurs are not big risk takers, they are calculated risk takers. Never risk it all on one venture.

Avoid the Cash Crunch

Nothing can diminish your enthusiasm for business more than a cash crunch. Being short on funds when the mortgage is due or when a supplier is supposed to be paid is the secret sad downside to being an entrepreneur. Not only can a shortage of funds hurt your business and your reputation, but it can wreak havoc on your marriage and family. If you want to retain your sanity, protect your significant other, and keep the dream alive, you must beware the cash crunch.

Usually, a cash shortage is the result of poor planning. In the beginning of your venture, you cannot be faulted for not knowing when money will come in the door, but as you proceed there should be no excuse for not planning accordingly. You must know your business cycle and when money is supposed to come in the door, and budget for that. Having a cash reserve in the bank for the proverbial rainy day makes good business sense.

If you find that you consistently run short of funds, then it is time to do something fundamentally new. Essentially, your options include:

- *Give yourself a raise.* Successful entrepreneurs respect themselves and charge a fair price for their services. Because you are your own boss, you set the prices. Although you should be concerned that you will drive away clients if you do charge more than you have been, it is still worth a shot. If your fears are valid, you can always lower your prices again; but if your fears are ungrounded, you will be giving yourself a well-deserved raise and thus eliminate the cash crunch.

- *Receive your receivables.* When you allow someone to buy your product "net 30" (that is, payable 30 days after the purchase), you are essentially lending that person money. Permitting these people extra time beyond 30 days to pay for a purchase is a commonplace, yet easily correctable, mistake. Would your bank allow you an extra 60 days to pay your loan? Of course not. Your business should be run the same way. Always remember that receivables are the lifeblood of your business, representing your business's cash flow and liquidity. Getting your receivables current, therefore, can bring in immediate cash.

- *Get a loan.* Sometimes business owners just need a short-term infusion of cash to get things moving again or maybe a long-term note or a line of credit might help.

Good businesses, long-term success stories, are not beset by consist needs for large cash infusions. You want to run your business the same way. Plan appropriately, budget accordingly, pay your creditors and suppliers on time, build a good business credit rating, and you will avoid the cash crunch dilemma and build a solid business.

Succeeding in Business during Tough Times

When times get tough, what do you do? The best recourse is to remember what has worked best for you and fall back on that. The business jujitsu master knows his strengths and weaknesses. When weak, it is not the time to attack. Rather, it is the time to fall back and concentrate on that which you do best. Succeeding in business, even in uncertain times, is possible if you follow some of these tips.

Use your best recipe. After some trial and error, successful businesses figure out what works. After that happens, they do the same thing over and over again. It could be an ad that works, a sale that brings in customers, or a monthly seminar. Whatever it is, it is a "recipe" for success. You make your business dough by utilizing a successful business recipe. Repeating a successful formula is the hallmark of any well-run business, and it is what you should do in tough times.

Advertise, advertise, advertise. Advertising is one of the most important things a small business can do. All too often when times get tight, the advertising budget is the first thing slashed. That is a big mistake. Various entrepreneurs through the years have said that when hit with a cash crunch, they refused to scale back. In fact, they opine that the best way out of a tough time is to expand business, not contract it, and advertising is a big part of that.

Play good defense. Entrepreneurs like to play offense. They like to come up with new ideas and implement them. That's great, but if you don't have a good defensive scheme in place, it's easy to get blindsided. Good defense is a twofold process. First, it means having structures in place to protect you, most notably, insurance and incorporation. The second part of playing good defense is to avoid stupid mistakes.

Try, try again. The path of the small businessperson is not always an easy one. Growing a business often takes trial and error, followed by a few mistakes, a couple of bonehead moves, and then, maybe, a home run.

Get Advice

Business jujitsu works when you have a problem to overcome. But what if you just need a friendly ear; someone off of which to bounce some new ideas? As you go about setting up and running your business, you will likely find that you need advice about all sorts of various and sundry matters. Where do you get it, especially if you have set up the business without a partner? The answer is from a board of advisors. A board of advisors is an independent group whose purpose is to give you ideas and feedback about your business. Board members can be business associates, colleagues, customers—anyone whose advice you will trust. Having people around who can give you a different perspective can be invaluable.

When looking for board members, you will want people:

- *Who are strong.* You don't want a rubber stamp. The whole purpose of a board of advisors is to give you a second (and third!) opinion. Getting some honest feedback can only help your business.
- *Who have different skills.* Even the best entrepreneurs only have some of the skills necessary to run a great business. Having board members who complement your skills can create a positive, synergistic effect. Similarly, having board members with skills and backgrounds different from one another can give your board an even broader base.
- *Who are experienced.* It is not uncommon when looking for outside funding that potential investors and bankers will call your board of advisors. When they do, it is far better if they find some experienced businesspeople and not your best friend from high school.

Board members are often compensated for their time, either with money or stock, although some are willing to assist for free. Those folks do it because they welcome the chance to be involved in a start-up. Sharing what they know and watching the company grow is pay in itself.

Another good thing about creating a board is that it can help you build credibility in the business world. A strong board full of professionals and businesspeople indicates that you have contacts and can take criticism.

The Work-Life Balancing Act

Finally, business jujitsu requires balance. It is very easy for new businesspeople to become consumed by work. Even though you might think your new business is all you can concentrate on right now, it is also important to remember that, however trite it might sound, there is more to life than business. Losing your balance can lead to burnout, marital problems, health problems, and business setbacks. If you don't strike a balance, you may come to resent your business.

What is a balanced life, exactly? There are probably as many definitions as there are people, but a simple way to look at it is to imagine your life as a pie chart cut into six equal pieces. The six slices represent the following:

1. *Your new business.* You already understand the importance of this slice of the pie.
2. *Your family and friends.* It is imperative that you spend enough time with your loved ones.
3. *Leisure time.* Balance means that you take time out to go to the movies, watch a game, hang out, play with the kids, or otherwise do those things that are fun for you.
4. *Physical and mental health.* It is easy when you are in business for yourself to be so stressed about time that you let your exercise routine and eating habits falter. But one reason you go into business for yourself is that it frees you up to do what you want. This is one of those places where you should take advantage of that freedom.
5. *Personal enrichment.* You need to take classes, read a book, learn something new, listen to music, go to a concert or play, and stay involved. Business becomes a burden when it is the only thing in your life.
6. *Spirituality and religion.* Go to church or synagogue, meditate, take a walk—however you connect, keep with it.

Each one of these six areas need to be fulfilled if you want to have a life that is fulfilling. There is little point in creating a great business if you end up being married to it 24/7. If you can figure out in which areas you are lacking, you can start to rebalance your life. The important thing is to take the time to reflect on what is important to you. It is usually not until something is out of balance that it actually comes to our attention.

THE BOTTOM LINE

Knowing what may lie ahead may also help you prevent it. Business jujitsu requires that you take the challenges (and potential crises) that might come your way and turn them into your advantage. Be balanced, flexible, and positive. Turn it around. The more you try business jujitsu, the easier it will become. That way, when you really need it, your skills are honed and ready for action.

Resources You Can Use

The Essential Guide to Managing Corporate Crises: A Step-by-Step Handbook for Surviving Major Catastrophes
by Ian I. Mitroff (Oxford University Press, 1996).

Harvard Business Review on Crisis Management
(Harvard Business School, 2000).

Kauffman Center for Entrepreneurial Leadership
Ewing Marion Kauffman Foundation
816-932-1000
4801 Rockhill Road
Kansas City, MO 64110
<www.entreworld.org>

The United States Ju-Jitsu Federation
<www.usjujitsu.net>

You'd Better Have a Hose If You Want to Put Out the Fire: The Complete Guide to Crisis and Risk Communications
by Rene A. Henry (Gollywobbler Productions, 2001).

20

Business Success Secrets

At my Web site <www.MrAllBiz.com>, there is a free newsletter that we send out every other week called *Small Business Success Secrets!* In it, entrepreneurs like you share what they believe to be their best ideas for succeeding in business. Many of those ideas have been interspersed throughout this book. But unlike Einstein's elegant theory, $E=mc^2$, it is impossible to create a grand theory of business success because it depends on many unquantifiable variables. What follows are some of the most important.

Create a Winning Recipe

After some trial and error in your business, you will figure out what works best. Once that happens, you will want to do the same thing over and over again. This is your recipe for success. Just like a food recipe, a business recipe can be followed time and again to achieve the same result. In fact, some believe that that's why money is called dough; you make your dough by using a recipe. In your business, your business dough recipe could be:

- An ad that works
- A monthly mailer
- A sale that brings in customers
- A monthly seminar
- A stall at the Saturday public market

- A billboard
- Great locations
- Almost anything that works and can be duplicated

If you think about it, repeating a successful formula is the hallmark of any well-run business. Budweiser sponsors sporting events because it knows that it will sell more beer if it does. Sponsoring sporting events is a tried and true business recipe. It works time and time again. Microsoft too has a recipe. We might call it "tweak and put out a new edition of Windows every few years." Microsoft knows that if it does so, it will be able to predictably count on those sales. Hollywood does the same thing. Whereas no one knows for sure what movie people will like, Hollywood knows that it reduces the risk of failure if, for example, Tom Cruise or Julia Roberts stars in it. Getting a big name to star in a movie is a business recipe.

If your business is going to be a long-term success, you will need to do the same thing. What will your recipe be? You need to experiment and figure out what works best. After you do, long-term success will be much more likely if you reduce that thing, whatever it is, to a formula that you can repeat over and over again.

In his great book *The E-Myth: Why Most Small Businesses Don't Work and What to Do About It,* author Michael Gerber explains that many people go into business because they love something and want to make a living at it, a baker who loves to bake, for example. Gerber makes clear that what trips up the baker is that, while what he wants is to bake, being a business owner

■ Creating a Winning Recipe

1. Experiment. Try several different ways to bring in business and quantifiably measure the success of each.

2. Which one can be reduced to a tried-and-true formula? Pick that one and write down the recipe.

3. Try the recipe to see if the results are consistent.

4. If so, stick with it; if not, go back to Step 1.

demands that he be an entrepreneur, which many bakers are not. Gerber's solution is to have the business owner, to the extent possible, create an efficient system that allows the business to run without him, much as McDonald's is run. This allows the baker to concentrate on what he loves best, rather than what he does worst.

Creating a winning recipe is an extension of this philosophy. Finding and creating a business success formula, the essence of your recipe, reduces your risk, makes the business far more predictable, allows you to concentrate on finding new recipes, frees you up to do what you love, and altogether makes being an entrepreneur a more fun, less scary, endeavor.

Create Multiple Profit Centers

The problem for most small businesses is that they learn one good recipe, stick with it, run it into the ground, and never bother to figure out another one. The owner has learned only one method of making a buck. The problem with having just a single moneymaking formula is that it will inevitably be hit when the dreaded business cycle turns south.

Just like the economy, all businesses have a business cycle. The ice cream store sees sales spike in the summer and drop in the winter. Starbucks sees sales rise in the winter and drop in the summer. While experience will teach you, often the hard way, what your business cycle is, you can learn it much easier by speaking with people in your own line of work who have been around for a while.

Once you know what your business cycle is, either through research or the school of hard knocks, you will want to minimize its effects on your business. One of the best ways to do that is to create *multiple profit centers,* a term coined by Barbara Winter in her book, *Making a Living Without a Job.* The theory is essentially this: To succeed long-term in business, you need several recipes. You need to diversify your income.

A smart stock investor does just that. He knows not to buy just one stock. That stock may go up, but it may go down. Having more than one stock ensures that when one stock does go down, the likelihood of taking a big financial hit is remote. His income is diversified. Your business must diversify as well if you are going to last.

Your new profit center could either be another "division" of your business or simply a new product:

- Amazon.com took the new division route. Amazon.com began by selling books online. Now it sells everything. Why? When one of its businesses is slow, it is unlikely that another will be as well. Instead of the business suffering a cash crunch, the money continues to roll in.
- Starbucks introduced new products. Knowing that its business slumped in the summer, Starbucks began to sell slushy-type iced coffee drinks. That's a different profit center than hot coffee and reduces the impact of the company's seasonal business cycle.

A lawyer may want to add a divorce practice to her wills and estates practice. A car rental agency might want to sell cars in addition to renting them. A photographer can add portraits to his wedding portfolio. The important

---

✎ Creating Multiple Profit Centers

1. What is your main profit center? _____

2. Name ten possible offshoots from that profit center that you could start:

   _____

   _____

   _____

   _____

   _____

3. Reduce that list to the five most likely successes:

   _____

   _____

4. Which of those would be the easiest to start?_____

5. Implement the best idea and then go on to the next. Create several recipes, several profit centers.

thing is that you create several recipes so that you have a few different ways to bring in money.

Give Them What They Want

"Ask them what they want and then give them what they want" is a philosophy mentioned earlier that bears repeating. Think about the best businesses around—those businesses that provide a great service, where people want to work, and that make money for the owners, investors, and employees—and you will find one thing they share: They serve the market.

A business that does not fulfill a market need is a business that will not succeed. Whether yours is a small mom-and-pop operation or a large company with many employees, the lesson is the same. You must know to whom you are selling and what it is they want. Finding that out can be as simple as chatting with the people who come in your store or as complicated as hiring a market research firm to survey potential customers. Whatever your method,

■ **Real Life Example**

Of all e-commerce merchants, Amazon.com is the one that does it right. Amazon.com's founder and CEO Jeff Bezos has repeatedly stated that he endeavors to make Amazon.com the most customer-centric business in the world. What is it book buyers want? They want to look at the book, get recommendations, and get a good deal. Well, that's exactly what Amazon .com offers.

At Amazon.com, not only can you now see sample pages of books you are browsing, but the site offers recommendations of other books you might like based on what you are looking at, and it offers consistent discounts and free shipping. On every product page, Amazon.com tells you whether the item is in stock and when shipment can be expected. When you do make a purchase, its system immediately sends you an e-mail confirming your order and telling you when it expects to ship it. Then, when your order does ship, it sends you another e-mail with your tracking number. Amazon.com gives its customer exactly what the customer wants, and has made a lot of money doing so. It's a valuable lesson.

you must know what it is your customers are looking for and then give it to them. It's almost too simple, and that's the beauty of it.

Get Help

Franchisors like to say that while a franchisee might be in business for himself, he is not in business by himself; the franchisor is behind him, helping him succeed. But in reality, that is true for anyone starting a business. There are many people who are ready and willing to help you grow your business.

The Small Business Administration

The U.S. Small Business Administration (SBA), established in 1953, provides assistance to help Americans start, run, and grow their businesses. Each year, the SBA offers financial, technical, and management assistance to more than one million business owners. Its site, <www.sba.gov>, is a wealth of information.

The SBA also funds several nonprofit organizations, one of which is called Small Business Development Centers. SBDCs are found in most communities. They offer individual counseling, conduct seminars and training sessions, sponsor conferences, and, in general, assist anyone seeking advice about operating a business. You can find your local SBDC at <www.sba.gov/gopher/Local-Information/Small-Business-Development-Centers/>.

The Service Corps of Retired Executives (SCORE)

The Service Corps of Retired Executives is another nonprofit association funded by the SBA. It is dedicated to entrepreneur education, as well as assisting in the formation, growth, and success of businesses nationwide. In partnership with the SBA, SCORE volunteers call themselves "Counselors to America's Small Business." The group consists of both working and retired executives and business owners who donate their time and expertise as volunteer business counselors. Their mentoring is free of charge. Check it out at <www.score.org>.

Women's Business Center (WBC)

State-run WBCs are nonprofit organizations funded by the SBA. According to the WBC:

The U.S. Small Business Administration is doing more than ever to help level the playing field for women entrepreneurs, and the SBA's Office of Women's Business Ownership is leading the way.

OWBO promotes the growth of women-owned businesses through programs that address business training and technical assistance, and provide access to credit and capital, federal contracts, and international trade opportunities. With a women's business ownership representative in every SBA district office, a nationwide network of mentoring round-tables, women's business centers in nearly every state and territory, women-owned venture capital companies, and the Online Women's Business Center, OWBO is helping unprecedented numbers of women start and build successful businesses. At every stage of developing and expanding a successful business, the Office of Women's Business Ownership is here to counsel, teach, encourage, and inspire.

You can find out more by going to <www.onlinewbc.gov>.

Web Sites

There are numerous Web sites dedicated to helping entrepreneurs succeed. Among the best are Entrepreneur.com, Inc.com, Workz.com, and bCentral.com.

What this means is that you are not alone. When you have a question, when you need a friend, when times are tough, when you want to expand, there are people around ready to help you. You might be in business for yourself, but you need not be in business by yourself. Assistance awaits.

Seven Secrets of the Great Entrepreneurs

While the idea of being an entrepreneur may start with a flicker, it often grows very bright. Even so, the question remains: Why are some entrepreneurs more successful than others? Usually, it is because they know some things other entrepreneurs do not. Here are the seven secrets of the great entrepreneurs.

1. Be Willing to Take a Big Risk

Entrepreneurship is, as we have discussed, a risk. When you quit your job to start a new business, there is no guarantee it will succeed, let alone succeed wildly. Cookie stores were nonexistent when Debbie Fields opened her first one in 1977. Today, Mrs. Field's Cookies numbers more than 1,000 stores. You have to be willing to look like a fool to succeed.

If you are going to succeed wildly in your own business (and that is the idea), you too will need to take a risk. An intelligent, calculated gamble has the chance to hit big. Of course, it can also backfire, but that's why we play the game.

2. Dream Big Dreams

In the early 1950s, a young engineer named Douglas Englebart decided that rather than work for 5½ million minutes for someone else (the amount of time that would elapse before he would turn 65), he would rather use his career to benefit mankind. He wanted to help people solve problems; that was the need he thought he could fill.

Englebart had an epiphany. At a time when computers were machines the size of a room that were used primarily for number crunching and had no screens at all, and despite the fact that he knew next to nothing about them, Englebart saw a future where the computer could be an interactive tool, operated by "any kind of a lever or knob, or buttons, or switches you wanted." That vision so engrossed Douglas Englebart that he spent the next decade chasing that dream, before eventually becoming known as the father of the computer mouse.

No one will give you permission to be bold, but boldness is a requirement. As W.H. Murray wrote in *The Scottish Himalayan Expedition*:

> Until one is committed, there is hesitancy, the chance to draw back, always ineffectiveness. Concerning all acts of initiative (and creation) there is one elementary truth, the ignorance that kills countless ideas and splendid plans: that the moment one definitely commits oneself, then Providence moves too. All sorts of things occur to help one that would never otherwise have occurred. A whole stream of events issues from the decision, raising in one's favor all manner of unforeseen incidents and meetings and material assistance, which no man could have dreamed would have come his way. I have learned a deep respect for one of Goethe's couplets: "Whatever you can do, or dream you can, begin it. Boldness has genius, power, and magic in it."

3. Value the Customer above All Else

For Richard Branson, founder of the Virgin Group, the customer is king. For instance, he believed that many record stores suffered because the shopping experience was boring and the staff needed to enjoy their jobs more. Voilà! Virgin Megastore was born—a place stocked to the brim that has a great vibe where you can usually listen to the music you want *before* you buy it. It might help to know too that Branson started out not much different than the rest of us. His first business was a record store above a shoe shop in London, and he bartered for his rent.

As Sam Walton put it: To succeed you need to exceed your customers' expectations. "Let them know you appreciate them. Make good on all your mistakes, and don't make excuses—apologize. Stand behind everything you do. The two most important words I ever wrote were on that first Wal-Mart sign, 'Satisfaction Guaranteed.' They're still up there, and they have made all the difference."

4. Take Care of Your People

This includes your employees, your investors, and your stockholders. In 1913, Henry Ford said, "The wages we pay are too small in comparison with our profits. I think we should raise our minimum pay rate." Moreover, eight years later Ford introduced the first five-day work week, stating, "Every man needs more than one day for rest and recreation." And if ever there was an entrepreneur who knew how to succeed, it was Ford.

5. Persevere

As I said, entrepreneurship is a risk and, as such, entrepreneurs often fail. Many successful entrepreneurs go bankrupt before they hit it big, but they stick with it anyway. In 1975, Microsoft's revenues were $16,000 and it had three employees. In 1976, revenues were $22,000 with seven employees. In both years, the company posted losses. Many companies would have quit after two such years, but most companies are not Microsoft.

6. Believe in Yourself

Buckminster Fuller, inventor of the geodesic dome and countless other tools, was an unknown, unhappy man when he decided to kill himself in

1927. But before he went through with it, he realized his problem had always been that he listened to others instead of himself. Then and there, he decided to trust his own intuition. Before he died, Fuller had revolutionized such disparate fields as architecture, mathematics, housing, and automobiles.

7. Have a Passion

A trait common to all great entrepreneurs is that they are passionate about what they do. Legendary investor and entrepreneur Charles Schwab put it this way, "The person who does not work for the love of work but only for money is not likely to make money nor to find much fun in life." Similarly, Anita Roddick, founder and managing director of Body Shop International, once said, "I want to work for a company that contributes to and is part of the community. I want something not just to invest in, I want something to believe in."

In the end, maybe writer Joseph Campbell said it best, "If you follow your bliss, doors will open for you that wouldn't have opened for anyone else." That is the job before you—to find that bliss and turn it into profit. A challenge? Yes. But what a great challenge it is.

The good news is that you need not be a world famous entrepreneur to think and act like one, and you need not reinvent the wheel either. Take from this book the ideas that you like, discard those you don't, become a great entrepreneur in your own right, and go conquer your part of the globe. Good luck!

THE BOTTOM LINE

Creating multiple profit centers is one of the smartest things you can do to ensure the long-term viability of your business. So is giving people what they want. Help is always nearby via the SBA and its affiliates. Finally, remember that boldness has genius, power, and magic in it.

Resources You Can Use

SBA Answer Desk

800-UASK-SBA (800-827-5722)
6302 Fairview Road, Suite 300
Charlotte, NC 28210
e-mail: answerdesk@sba.gov

Small Business Development Centers

202-205-6673
Office of Women's Business Ownership
Small Business Administration
409 Third Street, SW, Fourth Floor
Washington, DC 20416
e-mail: owbo@sba.gov
<www.sba.gov/gopher/Local-Information/Small-Business-Development-Centers/>

References

Books

The Big Idea: How Business Innovators Get Great Ideas to Market by Steven D. Strauss (Dearborn, 2001).

Blue's Clues for Success: The 8 Secrets Behind a Phenomenal Business by Diane Tracy (Dearborn, 2002).

The E-Myth Revisited: Why Most Small Businesses Don't Work and What to Do About It by Michael E. Gerber (Harper Business, 1995).

Guerrilla Marketing: Secrets for Making Big Profits from Your Small Business by Jay Conrad Levinson (Mariner Books, 1998).

Own Your Own Corporation: Why the Rich Own Their Own Companies and Everyone Else Works for Them by Garrett Sutton, Robert T. Kiyosaki, and Ann Blackman (Warner Books, 2001).

Portraits of Success: 9 Keys to Sustaining Value in Any Business by James Olan Hutcheson (Dearborn, 2002).

Small Time Operator: How to Start Your Own Business, Keep Your Books, Pay Your Taxes, and Stay Out of Trouble (Small Time Operator, 25th Edition) by Bernard B. Kamoroff (Bell Springs Publishing, 2000).

Successful Business Planning in 30 Days: A Step-by-Step Guide for Writing a Business Plan and Starting Your Own Business by Peter J. Patsula (Patsula Media, 2000).

The Upstart Small Business Legal Guide by Robert Friedman (Dearborn, 1998).

What No One Ever Tells You About Starting Your Own Business: Real Life Start-Up Advice from 101 Successful Entrepreneurs by Jan Norman (Upstart Publishing, 1999).

Magazines and Newspapers

Black Enterprise
<www.blackenterprise.com>

Business 2.0
<www.business2.com>

Business Startups
<www.entrepreneur.com>

Business Week
<www.businessweek.com>

Entrepreneur
<www.entrepreneur.com>

Fast Company
<www.fastcompany.com>

Forbes
<www.forbes.com>

Fortune
    <www.fortune.com>

Franchise Handbook
    <www.franchise1.com>

Harvard Business Review
    <www.harvardbusinessonline.com>

Inc.
    <www.inc.com>

Red Herring
    <www.redherring.com>

Wall Street Journal
    <www.wsj.com>

Other Web Sites

- <www.MrAllBiz.com>
- <business.lycos.com>
- <smallbusiness.yahoo.com>
- <www.aarpsmallbiz.com>
- <www.about.com/smallbusiness/>
- <www.asbdc-us.org>
- <www.att.sbresources.com>
- <www.bcentral.com>
- <www.bizland.com>
- <www.bloomberg.com>
- <www.business.gov>
- <www.busop1.com>
- <www.chamberbiz.com>
- <www.entreworld.com>
- <www.isquare.com>
- <www.onlinewbc.gov>
- <www.quicken.com/small_business/>

- <www.sba.gov>
- <www.score.org>
- <www.usatoday.com/money/smallbusiness/front.htm>
- <www.winwomen.org>
- <www.workz.com>

Associations

American Association of Home Based Businesses
Fax: 301-963-7042
P.O. Box 10023
Rockville, MD 20849
<www.aahbb.org>

American Small Businesses Association
800-942-2722
8773 IL Route 75E
Rock City, IL 61070

Home Business Institute
561-865-0865
P.O. Box 480215
Delray Beach, FL 33448
<www.hbiweb.com>

Marketing Research Association
860-257-4008
1344 Silas Deane Highway, Suite 306,
Rocky Hill, CT 06067
<www.mra-net.org>

National Association of the Self-Employed (NASE)
800-232-NASE (800-232-6273)
P.O. Box 612067
DFW Airport
Dallas, TX 75261-2067

National Business Association
800-456-0440
5151 Beltline Road, Suite 1150
Dallas, TX 75254
<www.nba.org>

National Retail Federation
202-783-7971
325 7th Street, NW, Suite 1000
Washington, DC 20004
<www.nfr.com>

National Small Business United
Phone: 202-293-8830
Fax: 202-872-8543
1156 15th Street, NW, Suite 1100
Washington, DC 20005
<www.nsbu.org>

U.S. Chamber of Commerce
202-659-6000
1615 H Street, NW
Washington, DC 20062-2000

Index

About the Author

Steven D. Strauss is one of the world's leading entrepreneur experts. A nationally recognized lawyer, columnist, and speaker, Steve's weekly column for USA Today.com is among the most widely syndicated columns on the Internet. He is also the owner of the Strauss Law Firm. Steve has received degrees from UCLA (B.A.), the Claremont Graduate School (M.A.), and the McGeorge School of Law (J.D.).

A highly sought after commentator and media guest, Steve has been featured on CNN, CNBC, *World Business Satellite,* Bloomberg Television, *The O'Reilly Factor,* MSNBC, Court TV, the BBC, and ABC News.

Steve has lectured around the world, including at the United Nations, on entrepreneurship, franchising, and business issues. You can contact Steve to speak to your group or sign up for his free newsletter, *Small Business Success Secrets!,* at his business Web site <www.MrAllBiz.com>.

Spread the Entrepreneurial Spirit

For special discounts on
ten or more copies of
The Business Start-Up Kit,
call Dearborn Trade Special Sales
at 800-621-9621, ext. 4410,
or e-mail rowland@dearborn.com.
You'll receive great service and
top discounts.

For added visibility,
consider private labeling
of books with your
organization name and logo.
We will also help you
identify speakers to make
your next event a
huge success.

Dearborn™
Trade Publishing
A **Kaplan Professional** Company